John Rowland West

Parish sermons for the advent and Christmas seasons

John Rowland West

Parish sermons for the advent and Christmas seasons

ISBN/EAN: 9783741106385

Manufactured in Europe, USA, Canada, Australia, Japa

Cover: Foto ©Thomas Meinert / pixelio.de

Manufactured and distributed by brebook publishing software (www.brebook.com)

John Rowland West

Parish sermons for the advent and Christmas seasons

PARISH SERMONS

FOR THE

Advent and Christmas Seasons.

BY THE
REV. J. R. WEST, M.A.,
VICAR OF WRAWBY.

LONDON:
J. MASTERS AND CO., 78, NEW BOND STREET.
MDCCCLXXV.

LONDON:
PRINTED BY J. MASTERS AND CO.,
ALBION BUILDINGS, BARTHOLOMEW CLOSE, E.C.

PREFACE.

THE all-absorbing subject for our thoughts during the Advent Season must be, of necessity, the First Coming of GOD in the Flesh. Thoughts of the Second Advent of the LORD from Heaven will come in only incidentally, as they may be suggested to us by the humility of His first Appearance.

Some indeed have been accustomed to begin the Christian year with four weeks' consideration of our LORD's Second Advent. But this is evidently a mistake; this is void of all propriety of arrangement; this is to invert the Order of our Sacred Year; this is to miss the very design for which the Advent Season is appointed.

Bishop Sparrow in his "Rationale of the

Prayer Book," writes thus of the Advent Sundays: "The principal Holy Days, as Christmas, Easter, and Whitsun Day, have some days appointed to attend upon them, as it were, to wait upon them, for their greater solemnity.

" Before Christmas are appointed four Advent Sundays, so called because they are to prepare us for CHRIST's Advent or Coming in the Flesh; forerunners to prepare for it and point to it."

To the same effect Bishop Jolly writes in his " Sunday Services:" " The Church, in order to raise our low thoughts and excite us to rejoice with fear and reverence (at Christmas time), unites with the meanness of His First Advent the majesty of His Second."

L'Estrange, in his " Alliance of Divine Offices," says: " The Church hath assigned to this great Festival (Christmas) the four Sundays preceding, which are, as it were, one Christmas Eve, and are therefore called Advent Sundays, as forespeaking CHRIST's Birthday."

The Advent Season is therefore certainly

intended to be preparatory to the Celebration of the Nativity of the LORD from Heaven in our Human Family. For the Church measures her Sacred Year, not by the motion of the natural sun in the sky, but by the course of our LORD's life, from His Nativity to His Ascension. The Church therefore must begin her Sacred Year of Holy Solemnities with the Rising of the Sun of Righteousness. The Advent Season preceding the Nativity, is the Twilight foretelling the approach of the Sun, which is just about to arise " with healing in His wings."

During the Advent Season therefore, we should put ourselves back into former ages, and consider ourselves as waiting for the Coming of the long-promised Messiah, expecting the Manifestation of GOD in the Flesh; we should diligently read the prophecies of the Messiah and of His Kingdom; we should ponder in our hearts the proper Advent Psalms (especially 45, 72, and 110), and thus seek to prepare ourselves more and more worthily every year for the celebration of that most stupendous event, when the Eternal SON of GOD was born into this world, made the Son of Mary.

For this is the infinitely great and glorious event in the history of our race, which changes everything to us, which makes all things new, introducing a new order of things amongst us.

For the Incarnation of the Eternal Word, the Advent of the LORD from Heaven, the Birth of the Second Adam, is the beginning of a New Creation. The manifestation of GOD in the Flesh is the mystery of mysteries which should therefore absorb all our best thoughts during the Advent Season.

CONTENTS.

Contents.

SERMON I.

THE BEGINNING OF THE YEAR CHANGED.

First Sunday in Advent.

Exodus XII. 2.

"This month shall be unto you the Beginning of months; it shall be the First Month of the Year to you."

THE fulness of the time was now come when God would redeem His people Israel out of their fallen state in Egypt, and restore them to their native land of Canaan.

This mighty and miraculous redemption would be a new era in their history. At their passage through the Red Sea old things would pass away, all things would become new. Their whole future history would date its beginning from this redemption; this would be the new foundation of all their institutions; this would form the new groundwork of all their worship.

B

The very style and order of reckoning time was
to be changed. By Divine Institution their
times and seasons were no longer to be measured by the old reckoning, but from a new
beginning. GOD commanded that no longer
the month Tisri, but the month Abib, in which
their redemption took place, should be for their
future history the Beginning of the Year; that
is, this should be the First Month of their
Ecclesiastical or Sacred Year; so that all their
Religious Observances and Holy Seasons should
be measured and dated from this new era, this
New Beginning of their history.

The month Tisri was still reckoned the beginning of their civil year for all secular purposes, but Abib was the New Beginning of time
for all the Holy Seasons and Sacred Festivals
which GOD instituted for them.

Now all things that happened to the Israelites in their redemption out of Egypt, and in
their forty years' journey to the Promised
Land, were so ordered by Divine Providence
as to form the great leading type or parable of
the Old Testament, in order to prefigure all
that was to come in our infinitely greater redemption. "All these things," (S. Paul expressly writes,) "happened unto them for en-
samples," that is, "types." (1 Cor. x. 11.)

When therefore the Great Future came,

which had been prefigured and promised all along from the first moment of the Fall; when all the ancient types were fulfilled by the actual Advent of the LORD the Messiah; when the fulness of the time again came; when GOD sent forth His SON to redeem us from the curse of our fallen state, to work the greatest of all His great miracles for us, to create all things new for us, to begin a new history of mankind; surely it was meet and right that the beginning of the year should be changed for us, and that the Church of CHRIST should reckon her times and seasons from the New Era, so that the Beginning of her Sacred Year should be different to that of the civil year.

In the kingdom of our earthly Sovereign indeed we still keep up the old reckoning of time; but in the Kingdom of CHRIST we reckon time from a new date.

As members of the First Adam, we reckon times and seasons by the revolutions of the natural sun in the sky; but as members of the Second Adam, GOD Incarnate, we reckon from a New Beginning, and divide our Christian Year into Holy Seasons, according to the Life of the SON of GOD in the Flesh. For He is the Sun of our Holy Year, and it is His Rising which begins it.

The Advent of GOD in the Flesh, brethren,

this truly began a new era for us. The Incarnation of the Second Person of the Godhead, this it is which did indeed begin a New Creation for us. For in Christ, the Second Adam, we are a New Creation, as it is written, " If any man be in Christ, he is a New Creature; old things are passed away, behold, all things are become New." (2 Cor. v. 17.)

The very beginning of the year is therefore changed for us. Now we measure time from the Advent of God in the Flesh. Now we infinitely prefer the Christian Year, and observe all its sacred Seasons with holy worship before God.

Let us also here call to mind the Divine Institution of "the New Moons" under the Jewish Law.

The moon is that heavenly body which is always a type or figure of the Church. For as the moon has no light of her own, but reflects the light of the sun; and as she is ordained to rule over the night during the sun's absence; and as she is continually waxing or waning, yet ever the same; so it is also with the Church, which is divinely constituted for us in the absence of our Lord, "having the Glory of God" in her. (Rev. xxi. 11.)

The New Moons were distinguished, under the Jewish dispensation, by peculiar sacred solemnities, typical of that new constitution of the Church which should take place at the Coming of the LORD, proclaiming beforehand the Gospel of the Kingdom of Heaven.

For at the Advent of the LORD, the Messiah, the Church of GOD entered into a new phase and received a new constitution in Him the Incarnate Word.

The great Prophet prophesied of this change in the Church in the times of the Messiah, saying, "Thou shalt be called by a New Name, which the mouth of the LORD shall name." (Isa. lxii. 2.) For when the LORD from heaven was made the Second Adam, the Church also was created in Him, to be one with Him, the true Eve, His Spouse, His Mystical Body. Then her New Name was revealed, "the Body of CHRIST," or "the Spouse of CHRIST." When He Himself received a New Name, His Church also received a New Name.

The New Moons continually signified this new constitution of the Church which would take place at the Coming of the LORD GOD. And so, at every Advent Season, we may say we fulfil the ancient type, we keep up in spirit the holy solemnity of the New Moon. We still observe the rising of the New Moon with a holy season; we celebrate the new constitution of the Church in the LORD Incarnate; we

begin all afresh in the course of our annual
solemnities in the Church of CHRIST,—even
from the descending to the ascending of the
LORD Incarnate.

Every week also, let us remember, begins
with a new beginning in the Church of CHRIST.
The ancient Sabbath of the old Creation has
passed away, and in its stead has come the
LORD's Day, the true Sun Day, the Day of the
Rising of our true Sun ; when Light was again
brought out of darkness, and Life out of death,
and Order out of confusion ; when the New
Man, even the LORD Incarnate, arose from the
dead in His Spiritual Body, the First-fruits of
our restored humanity, bringing life and immortality to light, making that Day to be the
First Day of the New Creation.

This is the Day that the LORD Himself hath
made, shining in the eyes of Faith with a most
glorious triple light ; the Day in which we
rejoice with a hope full of glory.

Now therefore, S. Paul writes, " Let no man
judge you in meat or in drink, or in respect of
a holy day, or of the New Moons, or of the
Sabbath Days, which are a shadow of things
to come : but the body is of CHRIST." (Col.
ii. 16.)

For now the shadow has passed by, and the
substance is come ; now all things are made

new; now all former typical and preparatory ordinances are fulfilled in the Kingdom of CHRIST, and are carried on and changed into their very and true Antitypes.

Now all holy rites and seasons are newly constituted in the Church of CHRIST. Now every year begins with Advent, and every week with Sunday. Now all our holy seasons begin from a New Beginning; all of them belonging to that New Creation which began with the Incarnation of the Eternal Word, and which still ever consists in Him; in and by which the Power and the Wisdom and the Love of GOD will be ever manifested unto all the Heavenly Hosts throughout eternity. (Eph. iii. 10.)

SERMON II.

THE SENDING FORTH OF GOD'S ETERNAL SON.

First Sunday in Advent.

GAL. IV. 4.

"WHEN THE FULNESS OF THE TIME WAS COME, GOD
SENT FORTH HIS SON."

THE annual course of services in the Church,
as you all know, brethren, is regulated by the
order of our SAVIOUR's Life. For He is the
true Sun; the true Light of the world. As
He said Himself; "I am the Light of the
world: he that followeth Me shall not dwell in
darkness, but shall have the Light of Life."

GOD manifest in the flesh, brethren, is the
true Light of the world. He is the Sun of our
Christian Year; regulating all our holy seasons; ever dividing the light from the darkness. So that every member of the Church
who follows this course, with serious attention

and earnest prayer, will not be walking in the darkness of Nature, but will be gaining, more and more, the light of Life : increasing in the knowledge of GOD and of JESUS CHRIST whom He hath sent.

For by this means, the Church continually keeps before our attention all those great events in our SAVIOUR's life, on which all the great Articles of our Christian Faith depend ; each in its proper order ; from His Descending to His Ascending : from His most lowly Nativity in the cattle-stall of Bethlehem, to His most triumphant Ascension to the Throne of His Kingdom.

Thus every attentive member of the Church, it is plain, has the best means given him for increasing in the knowledge of GOD and of our SAVIOUR JESUS CHRIST.

For I need hardly remind you, brethren, that in the matter of Religion we require nothing new. We require no new Church: no new Bible; no new Sacraments; no new Article of Faith.

What we do all require is this; that we should give more earnest heed to those great Articles of Faith which GOD has set before us : ever bearing in mind those words of the Apostle: "If any man think that he knoweth anything ; he knoweth nothing, yet, as he ought to know."

In this spirit of humility, then, brethren, let us all be thankful to the sparing mercy and the long-suffering goodness of God, that we are all here this day; that we are permitted to begin again; at this beginning of the Christian Year.

Do you not often feel, brethren, that you have great need to begin all over again? It is very often the best thing we can do. It is very often the only thing we can do, if we wish to save our souls alive. We should ever be of the same mind with S. Paul; ever forgetting all that is behind; ever making fresh beginnings; just as though we had utterly failed hitherto.

O how great is the patience and the forbearance and the goodness of God, in permitting us to do this; in putting up with this; in giving us opportunities for this; yea, even in helping and blessing us in this: if we do indeed seek Him with fresh earnestness; if we will indeed make a new beginning.

The first great event which the Church celebrates, at the beginning of her Christian year, brethren, is, of course, the Advent of the Lord from Heaven. The first Coming of the long-promised Redeemer of the world; the Incarnation of the Eternal Word; the Manifestation of God in the flesh; the Birth of the Lord

from Heaven in our human family, when the
SON of GOD became the Son of the Blessed
Virgin Mary. This, brethren, is the infinitely
great event, this is the profound Mystery, this
is the Miracle of all miracles, this is the very
wonder of eternity to which the Church would
direct all our best thoughts, during this season
of Advent.

Let us then now take the words of the text
for our guide, on this great and glorious Mystery of our Faith.

The holy Apostle writes: "When the fulness of the time was come." The foreknowledge and the wisdom of GOD are infinite. None
of His works are done of a sudden; but only in
the fulness of their proper times; only according to the Eternal purpose of His sovereign
will.

And so, therefore, before GOD would do this
New Thing, His infinitely great and most marvellous Work, He prepared the world for it, by
a long series of promises and types and prophecies.

The faith of all believers in GOD, all along,
from the very fall of man, rested on this great
promise of GOD, that a Second Adam should
be born, who should be the Redeemer of the
world. The great Prophets of GOD all prophesied concerning Him that should come; they

foretold the glory of His Advent, and they described the greatness of His Kingdom. And so all believers in GOD waited, in the patience of faith, for the fulfilment of this, GOD's great promise.

It seemed a long time to wait; generation by generation; for four thousand years. But the times and the seasons were all ordered in Divine Wisdom, and were all preparing the world for the Coming of the promised Messiah. For, "Wisdom reacheth from one end to another mightily; and sweetly doth she order all things." (Wisd. viii. 1.) At last, therefore, the fulness of the appointed time came: the great future promised from the beginning came: GOD began to fulfil His promise; GOD began His New Creation. GOD said, "Behold, I make all things new."

Now GOD's first creation of man in Adam, was great and marvellous. But GOD's second creation of man in the second Adam, was far more great and marvellous still. For GOD did not create the Second Adam out of the dust of the earth, as He did the First. But, when the fulness of the time was perfectly come, "GOD sent forth His SON," His Eternal and Co-equal SON, the Second Person of the ever-living Godhead, into this world; in order that He, even He, might be made our Second Adam, our Al-

mighty Redeemer, our Eternal Life and Glory.
He who had been in the glory of the FATHER
before the worlds were made, even "from everlasting," came down from that supreme height,
and condescended to take upon Himself our
created nature. He who had been from all
eternity in the form of GOD laid aside His Divine Glory, and was made in the form of man.
The Second Person of the all-glorious Godhead,
by whom all things were made, came down
from Heaven, and was incarnate by the HOLY
GHOST of the Blessed Virgin Mary, and was
made Man. "The Word was made flesh, and
dwelt among us," here below. The LORD from
Heaven was made the Second Man; the New
Head of the human race. He, the Eternal
SON of the FATHER, GOD of GOD, Light of
Light, very GOD of very GOD, of one Substance
with the FATHER, having Eternal Life in Himself, was thus sent forth into this world, "born
of a woman;" made the Son of the Blessed
Virgin Mary; whom all generations of Chris-
tians do therefore call " Blessed."

He Whose eternal throne is in the Light
unto which no man can approach, was openly
manifested here below, in the very truth of our
manhood; openly revealed to our mortal sight;
in exceedingly great humility, past all our
thoughts ; His human birthplace, a cattle-stall;

His cradle, a manger, borrowed from the ox
and the ass.

Into the infinitely gracious purposes of this
new work of GOD, brethren, the present time
does not permit us to enter. They are all however briefly expressed in the remainder of the
verse now before us; it was all done, in the
infinite love of GOD towards us, in order to
"redeem them that were under the law, that
we might receive the adoption of sons." All
the benefits of the Advent of the SON of GOD
into this world, the Apostle thus very briefly
comprehends in the two words, Redemption,
and Adoption; Redemption from the curse of
our fallen state; and Adoption into the family
of GOD's children again.

But let me now conclude, brethren, by asking you all to ponder more deeply in your
hearts than you have ever yet done this infinitely stupendous Mystery of our faith; the
very foundation of the Christian Religion: even
GOD Incarnate; GOD the Eternal SON, manifest
in the flesh; Whom the FATHER hath sent to
be the SAVIOUR of the world.

O ponder in your hearts, brethren, this most
amazing work of Divine Love towards us. O
think of the infinite glory thus conferred upon
our human race; that He Who made us should
Himself be born into our human family, and

so be made the Second Man, the New Adam;
for our eternal life and glory.

O prepare yourselves, brethren, this Advent
season, for the devout Celebration of Christmas
Day; that you may give all the honour you
can to our LORD's human Birthday. Do you
indeed believe in this great Mystery? Do you
believe in Him Whom the FATHER hath sent?
Then celebrate His Human Birthday with all
the reverence you can : show your faith in Him
in the midst of all His Human weakness and
poverty. O prepare yourselves to fall down
and worship Him as He presents Himself to
you on His most lowly throne, in the cattle-
stall; in that marvellous hiding of all His
Glory.

O do not prepare yourselves, brethren, to
spend Christmas as the world does: for if that
be all you make of Christmas, it is completely
lost upon you; it is all mere worldly self-
gratification; there is not any true Christian
faith, or any true Christian rejoicing in it.
Shall you have faith enough, do you think,
brethren, to enable you to fall down before that
Little Infant, lying in a manger, and to say to
Him, in profoundest reverence, " My LORD,
and my GOD?"

And remember, brethren, that not one single
person calling himself a Christian, can worship

the FATHER at Christmas-time, as he ought to do, if he does not worship Him in that most special of all acts of worship which His SON, our LORD, has Himself instituted for us, and commanded us all to unite in, continually, even till He come again in His Glory.

Are you, then, brethren, at all awake from sleep? Are you deeply pondering in your hearts the Mysteries of the Kingdom of GOD Incarnate? Are you listening to the voice of the tender mercy of GOD, in this season of His grace? In this little life between Heaven and Hell, are you corresponding with the gracious invitations of your SAVIOUR's Love? Are you yielding yourselves as those that are alive from the dead, unto Him Who is knocking at the door of your hearts?

I beseech you all, brethren, not to waste away and spoil this Advent season; but so to awake, so to prepare yourselves to receive your SAVIOUR, now that He presents Himself to you in the meekness, in the lowliness of His first Advent, that you may not be consumed with terror, as in a moment, when He comes again down from Heaven; not lying in a manger, but seated on the Throne of His glory; not attended by the humble shepherds, but by all the armies of Heaven : not to seek and to save that which is lost, but to be the Judge of all mankind; in flaming fire to take vengeance on those of us who know not GOD and obey not His Gospel, but to be glorified in His Saints, and to be admired for ever in all them that believe.

SERMON III.

THE GREAT MYSTERY OF GODLINESS.

First Sunday in Advent.

1 TIMOTHY III. 16.

"GREAT IS THE MYSTERY OF GODLINESS; GOD WAS MANI-
FEST IN THE FLESH."

THE Mysteries of GOD, brethren, in His creation around us, are great and manifold. But
the Mysteries of GOD in CHRIST are far more
great and marvellous still.

The smallest seed, the meanest insect, con-
tains in it a great mystery of life,—a mystery
of the power of GOD, past our finding out.
What then, brethren, can we think,—what shall
we say of this, which is "the great mystery
of godliness;" GOD's greater work; the miracle
of all miracles; the very amazement of eternal
ages; "GOD Himself manifest in the flesh."

The Mysteries of Nature belong to the creature; this belongs to the Creator Himself. This Mystery is therefore great beyond all our thoughts; it is unsearchably great and infinitely marvellous.

Consider what it is. The *first* great Mystery of the Christian Revelation is this, that in One Eternal Godhead there are Three Persons, of One Substance, Power, and Eternity,—the FATHER, the SON, and the HOLY GHOST.

The *next* great Mystery of the Christian Revelation is this,—that the Second Person of the One Eternal Godhead has been made Man. This is the great "Mystery of godliness," of which our text speaks, "GOD was manifested in the flesh." Or as S. John writes in the beginning of his holy Gospel, "In the beginning was the Word, and the Word was with GOD, and the Word was GOD: and the Word was made Flesh, and dwelt among us." And also, in the beginning of his Epistle,—"That which was from the beginning, which we have heard, which we have seen with our eyes, which we have looked upon, and our hands have handled, of the Word of Life; for the Life was manifested, and we have seen It, and bear witness, and show unto you that Eternal Life which was with the FATHER, and was manifested unto us."

"For in the fulness of the time, GOD sent

forth His Son into this world." As at this
season of the year He was born into our human
family,—the Eternal Son of God was made
the Son of the Blessed Virgin Mary,—so that
two whole and perfect Natures, that is to say,
the Godhead and the Manhood, were joined
together in One Person, never to be divided.

As in ourselves the reasonable soul and flesh
is one Man, so God and Man is one Christ.
He whose new Name is "Jesus," is thus,
brethren, perfect God and perfect Man.

This great Mystery, brethren, is our grand
Glory. This is the very root and foundation
of all our Christian faith and of all our Christian hope. Its greatness is infinite and eternal,
—far beyond all our knowledge, far above all
our thoughts. The Creator of all things has
taken upon Himself our created nature. God
and Man are for ever joined together, in the
Person of the Incarnate Son.

Consider therefore, brethren, how infinitely
great the consequences of this stupendous
Mystery must be.

The Advent of God in the flesh could not
but affect all things mightily. So amazing an
event as the Incarnation of the Second Person
of the Eternal Godhead could not but produce
infinitely great consequences. O how often,
O how earnestly should we consider them.

I. Consider, brethren, the consequences as they relate to GOD Himself.

The Divine Nature is now united for ever to the Human. The greatness of this truth, brethren, is of course past all our thoughts. The Manhood and the Godhead are inseparably united. Now there lives and reigns in the supreme power and glory of the Throne of the Eternal Godhead, the Man, even the LORD JESUS.

So that by the Divine Incarnation the very Throne of the Godhead has become in some way changed. The doctrine of the Blessed Trinity can now no longer be held apart from the doctrine of the Divine Incarnation. Now we look up by faith into the Heaven of heavens, and there we behold JESUS. Now a Man lives and reigns in the glory of the FATHER; and that Man, the Second Person of the Godhead.

II. Next consider, brethren, how great must be the consequences of the Incarnation of the SON of GOD, as they relate to ourselves.

These are indeed so infinitely great that they will be the subject of our praise and adoration for all eternity.

It was a great glory for us, brethren, that Man should have been created in the likeness of GOD. But is it not a far higher and greater glory still, that when man had spoilt the glory

of his first creation in Adam, GOD the SON
should Himself be made in our Likeness, and
become to us a Second Adam ; so that we
being united to Him as members to a new
Life-giving Head, might be restored from all
the evils of the Fall, and lifted up even into His
Life and Glory?   For, in very few words, the
Divine Incarnation brings us a mighty deliver-
ance from all the evils of our fall in Adam, and
lifts us up even into the eternal glory of GOD.
The Second Person of the Godhead, by being
made Man, by His Advent in the flesh, by His
Birth into our human family, brings with Him
into our human family perfect remedies for all
our sad necessities, and opens to us an inconceivable exaltation, even into His own Eternal
Joy.

For now, He Who made us is not ashamed
to call us His Brethren.   Now are we related
to GOD, so as none other of His creatures are.

Who of us then can say, who of us can for
a moment conceive, what glories are yet to
spring, from the Manger, Cross, and Grave of
GOD's Eternal SON ?

Well then, brethren, may we exclaim,—
"O come, let us sing unto the LORD: let us
heartily rejoice in the strength of our salvation."

O may GOD grant unto us all that we may

indeed rejoice before Him for all eternity in the supreme glories of this mighty salvation. O let none of us be neglecting this great salvation which is now offered us. Let us all remember that this is our only allotted time for learning to believe in Him Whom the FATHER hath sent, for receiving this great Mystery into our hearts, for keeping the words of the SON of GOD, for preparing for the overwhelming glory of His Second Advent.

But let us not fail to ponder in our hearts at this holy season *the manner* in which GOD is wont to perform His great works.

Consider the manner in which GOD first of all openly revealed to us the stupendous Mystery of our faith, at the Advent of His SON from Heaven. One of the ancient prophecies clearly foretold this manner,—"He shall come down as the rain into a fleece of wool, even as the drops that water the earth." We might have thought that when GOD our SAVIOUR would be sent forth from Heaven, the doors of Heaven would be wide opened, and that He would come down in such open majesty that all the world would be forced at once to know Him to be the LORD of Glory.

But not so. The rain that makes the whole earth fruitful; the drops that water the face of the earth; with what gentleness, and silence,

and littleness do they come, so that not even
the tenderest herb is hurt thereby.

In like manner all the worlds of the Universe
roll in calm and silent grandeur around the
Throne of the Great Creator. In like manner
all the plants of the earth, all the lilies of the
field, all the mighty trees of the forest grow,
silently and imperceptibly, into all their strength
and beauty.

In like manner, when the LORD Incarnate
Himself did any great and good work in the
days of His Flesh, He made no noise about it,
as we so often do ; but took care to say, " See
that no man know it." Never once did He
break the bruised reed, nor ever once quench
the smoking flax.

Even such was the gentleness and the silence
and the humility of His First Coming amongst
us. Such was the manner of the Advent of
GOD our SAVIOUR.

O let us all then be greatly encouraged by
the exceeding great humility of His human
Birthday, to draw very near unto GOD our
SAVIOUR.

Let us all fall down in the dust, before His
lowly manger-throne, in deepest humility,—
smiting upon our breasts, crying for His mercy,
seeking for His saving Grace.

Let us confess Him GOD, even in all His

poverty, weakness, and littleness. Let us have a lively and steadfast faith in the great Mystery of Godliness. Let us all fall down and worship before the Eternal Son of God, manifest in the Flesh,—come from Heaven in all lowliness and gentleness,—come to bless, and comfort, and save every humble soul.

SERMON IV.

THE KINGDOM OF HEAVEN.

Second Sunday in Advent.

S. MATTH. III. 2.

"THE KINGDOM OF HEAVEN IS AT HAND."

THE prophets of old time all prophesied of our LORD as a King. They described the glory of His kingdom in the most striking and glowing terms. And in agreement with all the ancient prophecies, when the Archangel of Heaven announced to the Blessed Virgin Mary that she should be the mother of the long-promised Messiah, he said to her, "The LORD GOD shall give unto Him the throne of His father David; and He shall reign over the house of Jacob for ever, and of His kingdom there shall be no end."

Now the Jews firmly believed all these

ancient prophecies. They all believed that the promised Messiah would reign as a great King. They all expected that when He came He would set up a new kingdom ; because it is of necessity that every king has a kingdom. And this kingdom being given unto Him, not by man, but by God, they therefore commonly called it "the Kingdom of God," or "the Kingdom of Heaven," or sometimes simply "the kingdom."

When therefore S. John the Baptist gave that clear warning, "Repent ye, for the Kingdom of Heaven is at hand," they would all understand what he meant. They would not want any explanation. Very startling to them indeed would be the clear announcement, "the Kingdom of Heaven is at hand." It would mean in their hearts at once "The promised Son of David is born. The Lord, the Messiah, is come. The King of Israel is just about to set up His kingdom."

And when the Lord Himself began His public ministry, how strikingly did He repeat the Baptist's warning, saying, "The time is fulfilled, and the kingdom of God is at hand; repent ye, and believe the Gospel."

The Lord also commanded His Apostles to give the very same warning of the near approach of His Kingdom, saying, "As ye go, preach, saying, The Kingdom of Heaven is at hand."

This Kingdom of Heaven was then, therefore, nigh at hand, but it was not then actually come. The King Himself was then actually born into the world, and therefore His Kingdom was "at hand," because He could not be a King without a kingdom. To some of the people one day standing before Him our LORD said, "There be some standing here which shall not taste of death till they have seen the Kingdom of GOD come with power." Before those persons died, therefore, this Kingdom of Heaven did actually come, with power from on high.

When our LORD had overcome the sharpness of death and had ascended into Heaven, then "All power was given Him" of the FATHER, for His new Kingdom, both in Heaven and in earth. Then GOD the FATHER said unto His SON, appearing before Him in our manhood, "Sit Thou at My right hand." Then the LORD JESUS began to reign in Heaven above. Then the Son of Man sat in the throne of His glory. Then the great prophecy of Daniel was fulfilled, and the Son of Man received of the FATHER a Kingdom which shall never pass away. (Daniel vii. 13, 14.)

And upon the coming of the HOLY SPIRIT on the great Day of Pentecost, this Kingdom

began upon earth also. The LORD, the HOLY
GHOST, then opened the Kingdom of Heaven
upon earth to all believers, by the ministry of
S. Peter. That was the birthday of the Church
of CHRIST, the beginning of the Kingdom of
GOD Incarnate upon earth. For He Himself
had said, "Verily, verily, I say unto thee, except any one be born of water and of the
Spirit, he cannot enter into the Kingdom of
GOD;" and on that day the Sacrament of Regeneration was first administered. And this
kingdom has remained opened upon earth ever
since. In our Baptism, of water and the Spirit,
we entered into the same Kingdom of GOD
Incarnate.

Now therefore we no longer say, "The
Kingdom of Heaven is at hand," but "The
Kingdom of Heaven is come," with the power
of the HOLY GHOST; the King is reigning on
His throne in Heaven above, and His Kingdom reaches down to this earth, and we have
entered into it.

The Son of Man has now ascended into
Heaven; He is sitting in the throne of His
glory, having received of the FATHER a new
Kingdom, even the Kingdom of the Regeneration. And on the Day of Pentecost, upon the
first ministration of the holy Sacrament of
Regeneration, men below began to be made

members of a new Divine head, men below
began to be incorporated into the mystical
Body of the Second Adam, men below began
to be re-created in CHRIST JESUS, men below
began to be lifted up into the New Creation,
even into the Kingdom of the Regeneration.

Have you, brethren, an intelligent faith in
this mystery of GOD and of CHRIST?

Those people of Nazareth never discerned
the Presence of GOD Incarnate amongst them
all those years He lived there. So now, the
world does not discern the presence of the
Kingdom of Heaven amongst them: because it
is an object of faith rather than of sight.

Do you understand and believe, brethren,
that those words of the Baptist are now actually
fulfilled, " The Kingdom of Heaven is at
hand ?"

Do you understand that this new kingdom,
the Kingdom of the LORD GOD Incarnate, is
now no longer " at hand" but actually "come,"
with power of the HOLY GHOST; come down
from Heaven at the coming of the HOLY
GHOST; and that you, at your Baptism, have
entered into it?

Do you understand that the New Jerusalem,
the city of the living GOD, the Bride of CHRIST,
began to come down out of Heaven on that
day, having the glory of GOD in her, and

that you are now living in the New Jerusalem?

Do you believe in CHRIST only, apart from
His Kingdom, as many ignorantly do in these
days of religious darkness? As if He could
be a King and yet have no Kingdom! As if
there could be a King without a Kingdom
under His rule! As if any one could believe
rightly in CHRIST without believing in His
Church! As if we might stop, in the Apostles'
Creed, at the article, "I believe in the HOLY
GHOST," and not go on to the next, "I believe
in the Holy Catholic Church," which is the
Kingdom of CHRIST, the Kingdom of Heaven
upon earth.

It is doubtless a great matter, brethren, that
you should be living in the kingdom of England. But that is a mere passing trifle in comparison of this, that you are living in the
Kingdom of the LORD Incarnate, the New
Kingdom of Heaven.

Lastly, consider a moment, brethren, *on
what condition* do you continue to enjoy the
blessings and advantages of living in the kingdom of England? On the condition, of course,
that you obey the laws of the kingdom.

So in the Kingdom of the LORD CHRIST.
All its spiritual gifts and blessings are yours,
on condition that you live, or at least sincerely

strive to live, according to its laws. And what
are its essential laws? They are the very same
as the three Vows of our Baptism, on the very
condition of which you were entered into the
Kingdom, namely, Repentance, Faith, and
Obedience.

O let us all well consider this. Are you,
brethren, sincerely and earnestly striving,
through the Grace of CHRIST, your new Divine
Head, to live a life of true repentance and
of fruitful faith and of holy obedience?

You know, brethren, what a sure and certain
word of peace and comfort and blessed hope
I am authorized by CHRIST to declare and pronounce to all who truly repent and unfeignedly
believe the Gospel of the Kingdom; even the
absolution and remission of their sins; for the
precious Blood of CHRIST continually avails to
cleanse from all sin all such as are walking in
the light of the Gospel.

Are you then truly repenting of every sin?
Are you unfeignedly believing the Mysteries of
the Kingdom of Heaven? Are you keeping
the sayings of the LORD GOD? In one word,
Are you living, with all diligence, according to
your Baptism?

Now the Kingdom of GOD is with us, "without observation." To discern its presence is
now a trial of faith for all of us. But when

its glory is openly revealed, when the King appears sitting on His throne, then He will cast out of His Kingdom all workers of iniquity. Then at the majesty of His Second Advent, only they who now live in true repentance and faith will be able to stand.

and **Glory.**
he **FATHER**
from **ever-**
me **height,**
imself **our**
n from **all**
le **His Di-**
m of **man.**
Godhead,
ame **down**
the **HOLY**
, and **was**
flesh, **and**
LORD from
the **New**
e **Eternal**
Light of
Substance

rld, " **born**

of **Chris-**

the **Light**
was openly
th of

all

SERMON V.

THE KINGDOM OF HEAVEN.

Second Sunday in Advent.

S. Luke xxii. 29.

"I appoint unto you a kingdom, as My Father hath appointed unto Me."

The prophecies of old time, brethren, often spoke of the promised Messiah as a King. They often described the glory of the Kingdom which our Lord would set up at His Coming. The Jews therefore all expected that the promised Son of David would come as a King. So that they easily understood what S. John the Baptist meant, when he said to them: "Repent, for the kingdom of Heaven is at hand." For even at that moment the King of that kingdom was standing amongst them, though they knew Him not.

When the Lord Jesus ascended into the

glory of the FATHER, then His kingdom actually began in heaven above. For then the LORD, that is, GOD the FATHER, said unto our LORD, " Sit Thou on My right hand." Then, " All power was given unto our LORD in heaven and in earth." Then the LORD JESUS received of the FATHER a kingdom. Then He was given to be " Head over all things to the Church." Then the LORD JESUS began to reign as King, being crowned with all honour and glory. Then " the Son of Man sat in the throne of His glory."

And upon the coming of the LORD, the HOLY GHOST, on the great day of Pentecost, this Kingdom of the LORD JESUS actually began upon earth also. Then that Kingdom of Heaven of which the Baptist gave such clear warning, was no longer " at hand," but it actually came with power : then the Kingdom of CHRIST our LORD, the Kingdom of Heaven upon earth, the Kingdom of the Regeneration, was actually opened unto all believers. For the Apostles, being filled with the HOLY GHOST, went everywhere, and began the New Kingdom of GOD, joining men together in a new fellowship, baptizing them into one new Body by one Spirit.

But the King Himself was invisible : He was reigning on His Throne of Glory far above all the powers and principalities, all the thrones and dominions of Heaven.

How then was His Kingdom to be carried on and administered here upon earth beneath? Did our LORD make no provision for the government of His Kingdom upon earth? Did He give no power or authority to any one to rule in His Kingdom upon earth for Him? Let us consider our LORD's own words concerning this very point.

To the twelve Apostles He expressly said, "I appoint unto you a Kingdom, as My FATHER hath appointed unto Me." And again; "In the Regeneration, when the Son of Man shall sit in the throne of His glory, ye also shall sit upon twelve thrones, judging the twelve tribes of Israel."

It is plain, therefore, that our LORD did give express power and authority to the twelve Apostles to be the First Rulers of His Kingdom upon earth.

Let us also consider what is said concerning the foundation of the Church in Rev. xxi. 14. It is there said, that the Wall of the New Jerusalem, which is the Church of CHRIST, the Mystical Body of the Second Adam, the Bride of CHRIST, which began to come down out of Heaven, on the day of Pentecost, having the glory of GOD in her; the Wall of this City of the Living God (it is written) has "twelve foundations," and in them the names of the twelve Apostles of the Lamb.

To the twelve Apostles, then, brethren, it is plain, our LORD Himself gave power to be the first founders of His Kingdom upon earth. The Church is in a true and real sense built upon them.

Again, to S. Peter in particular, the first of the Apostles, our LORD said, " I will give unto thee the keys of the Kingdom of Heaven." And what is the use of a key ? To open or to shut the door; to admit, or to exclude. And that which the Divine Head of the Church gave first of all to S. Peter alone, He afterwards extended to all the twelve, saying; " Whatsoever ye shall bind on earth shall be bound in Heaven ; and whatsoever ye shall loose on earth shall be loosed in Heaven."

Their acts upon earth the King Himself said He Himself would ratify and confirm in Heaven.

Here, brethren, let us not fail to mark that the LORD appointed this Kingdom; He gave these spiritual powers, He assigned this spiritual authority, He committed the care and government of His Kingdom upon earth, not to any of the kings or princes of this world, but to twelve persons chosen by Himself from very humble stations in this world; the first or head of them being a fisherman, called from the sea of Galilee.

Thus, therefore, do we understand, in the most plain and striking manner, that the kingdom of CHRIST upon earth, in all its spiritual power and authority, is entirely independent of the Kingdoms of this world.

To whom did the LORD GOD Incarnate commit the keeping of the keys of His Kingdom upon earth? He gave them into the hands of a fisherman, called from the sea of Galilee. Could anything, brethren, more strikingly teach us that the Kingdom of CHRIST upon earth is entirely and absolutely independent of all the kingdoms of this world : it is a kingdom *in* the world, but not *of* the world.

CHRIST Himself, then, brethren, on His Ascension into Heaven, received of the FATHER a Kingdom.

And this His new Kingdom began upon earth on the day of Pentecost, and its government was committed into the hands of the twelve Apostles.

Next, we must consider, that this Kingdom, which our LORD appointed to the twelve Apostles, was intended to *remain* in the world, always, even to the end. This Kingdom of Heaven upon earth, thus at first committed to the charge of the twelve, was not to become extinct upon their decease, but to remain. And it has remained in the world to the present day.

On this point, that express promise which our LORD gave on the day on which He ascended to the Throne of His Kingdom is most absolutely plain and certain: for He then said to His Apostles, "Lo, I am with you alway, even to the end of the world." Alway, in every age, even to the end of the world, is the LORD mindful of this promise. Never does it fail. His Apostles therefore remain with us, and they continue in their office, in some true and real sense, "alway, to the end of the world:" and our LORD'S Presence is specially pledged to them, in all their spiritual acts.

The Church of CHRIST, built on the foundations of the twelve Apostles, has thus therefore remained in the world to the present day, and it will remain unto the end of the world; for the gates of hell cannot prevail against it, because GOD is in her midst.

For the Apostles took care, before they all left the world, to set the Church in order. They ordained others to succeed themselves, in the sacred offices of the Christian Ministry. Everywhere we find that the Church was set in order under Bishops, Priests, and Deacons. So that the Bishops are now sitting in the seats or thrones of the Apostles, and are the spiritual rulers of the Kingdom of CHRIST upon earth. So that our LORD's promise is thus continually receiving its fulfilment; the Apostles, in the persons of their successors, are sitting on their twelve thrones, ruling the twelve tribes of the true Israel. That is to say, that spiritual authority which our LORD gave to the Apostles to be Rulers of His Kingdom upon earth has been carried on from age to age in the persons of their successors.

To the Bishops of the Church are still committed the keys of the Kingdom of CHRIST. To them is still committed the administration of the Sacraments of CHRIST; without which there is no salvation promised to any of us.

Our LORD's appointment then, brethren, is most surely fulfilled amongst us to the present day. That Kingdom which our LORD appointed to the Apostles is still with us. The Kingdom of CHRIST reaches down from His Throne in Heaven, even unto us, and is amongst us, and is administered upon earth by the successors of the Apostles, always; and will be, " always, even to the end of the world."

Let us ever bear in mind, then, brethren, this great truth : that we are living in two Kingdoms : one, the Kingdom of England; the other, the Kingdom of Heaven. One is an earthly kingdom, of which our Queen is the Sovereign; the other, is a heavenly Kingdom, of which the ascended Lord Jesus is the King.

One we know by sight; the other we know by faith. Of one, we say, " we see it;" of the other, we say, " I believe in it;" " I believe in the Holy Catholic Church."

And let us make this the practical conclusion, viz. that our obedience is due to the rulers in both kingdoms.

Concerning our obedience to the rulers of the earthly Kingdom, it is plainly written; "Submit yourselves to every ordinance of man, for the Lord's sake; whether it be to the King, as supreme, or unto governors that are sent by him."

And, concerning our obedience to the spiritual Rulers in the Kingdom of Christ, the precept of the Word of God is equally plain and strong: " Obey them that have the rule over you, and submit yourselves; for they watch for your souls."

Thus is our obedience Divinely commanded, in both Kingdoms. Thus are we plainly bound to obey both our temporal and our spiritual rulers: both our Bishop and our Queen.

Under all ordinary circumstances, it is a great and open sin, to disobey either the secular authority of the State or the Spiritual authority of the Church.

There is now no necessity to dwell upon the duty of obedience to the secular authority of our earthly Sovereign : for all acknowledge that.

Let me only ask you, brethren, to consider now the duty of obedience to that Spiritual Authority which CHRIST has given to the Rulers of His Kingdom. For this is a duty which is not acknowledged by many in our day.

Could our LORD have set up a Kingdom in the world, without appointing certain rulers of it and giving to them certain spiritual powers ? Has He not expressly appointed this Kingdom to His Apostles and their successors, always, even to the end of the world ? And has not our LORD spoken, in the most strong way possible, of our duty to obey the authority of His Church, saying ; "If any man hear not the Church, let him be unto thee as a heathen." (S. Matth. xviii. 17.)

Very great and important therefore must be the duty of obedience to the spiritual authority of the rulers of the Church. For our LORD cannot forget His own institutions. He cannot act contrary to His own promises. He has solemnly said that what the rulers of the Church do for Him upon earth, according to His will, He Himself will confirm in Heaven above.

This then of necessity forms one part of the present trying of our faith : namely, whether we will believe in the presence of this Kingdom of Heaven amongst us, and obey its spiritual authority.

When CHRIST Himself was visibly present amongst those people in Judæa, it was a trying of them, whether they would believe in Him, or not. So the presence of His Kingdom amongst us now forms a part of our trial.

Many amongst us never discern this presence of the Kingdom of Heaven. They think only of the kingdom of England.

They believe in CHRIST: but they have no intelligent faith in the Kingdom of CHRIST. They think of Him, as of a King without a Kingdom! They think they have no other authority to obey than the secular authority of the temporal governor. They acknowledge no other king but Cæsar.

But consider, brethren, I beseech you, that " there is another King, one JESUS;" and that His Kingdom is amongst us; and that our obedience is due to the Spiritual Rulers of this Kingdom, by the express command of the King Himself; and that if there is any collision at any time between the rulers of this world and the rulers of the Kingdom of our LORD, we must obey the authority of His Kingdom rather than that of the other.

The Advent of the SON of GOD in the flesh

and the setting up of His New Kingdom amongst us creates for us of necessity a new sphere of responsibility.

It becomes one essential part of the trying of our faith, to acknowledge and to obey the authority of the Kingdom of CHRIST upon earth.

For the Church of CHRIST is a Divinely organised society, having in her the Power of Heaven; from which if any one be rightfully cut off, he has no hope of salvation, until he repents and is restored. The Church of CHRIST is Divinely organised, independently of the will of any earthly nation or kingdom, deriving her spiritual power from her Divine Head, not through any prince or government of this world, but through Peter the fisherman of Galilee.

In our own country, brethren, we have too long overlooked this vital truth. The State has almost absorbed the Church. The civil sword has too long hidden the Keys of the Kingdom of Heaven. The earthly glory of the Crown has too long eclipsed the heavenly glory of the Mitre. Even some of our Spiritual Rulers themselves have seemed content to rule by means of the secular power given them by Parliament, rather than by their own inherent spiritual authority. Our Church Synods have been silenced and chained by the secular government.

Now that our secular government is no longer of necessity even Christian, no faithful member of the Church can be ever satisfied with this state of things. For to yield the spiritual keys into the hands of the secular power, to let the princes of this world rule in the Kingdom of Heaven, this, surely, is to be unfaithful to Him Who is the King of the Kingdom; this, surely, is that horrible sin of spiritual harlotry which is so dreadfully condemned in the Word of Divine Revelation.

Awake then, brethren, I beseech you; awake to the presence of the Kingdom of Heaven. Act by faith in the Kingdom of the LORD JESUS, now existing amongst us. Obey its rulers, not because they happen to be members of Parliament, but because they have the keys of the Kingdom of Heaven; for the King of the Kingdom cannot make void His own ordinances. He cannot act contrary to His own promises.

It is as dangerous to us in our day to live in unbelief, as to the presence of the Kingdom of Heaven amongst us, as it was dangerous to the people of Judæa, in that day to live in unbelief, as to the presence of the King Himself.

The Advent of GOD in the flesh and the presence of His new Kingdom amongst us places us in a new sphere of being and of consequent responsibility.

SERMON VI.

THE KINGDOM OF HEAVEN.

Second Sunday in Advent.

S. MATTH. XI. 11.

"VERILY I SAY UNTO YOU, AMONG THEM THAT ARE BORN
OF WOMEN, THERE HATH NOT RISEN A GREATER THAN
JOHN THE BAPTIST; NOTWITHSTANDING, HE THAT IS
LEAST IN THE KINGDOM OF HEAVEN IS GREATER THAN
HE."

THIS is one of those sayings of the SON of
GOD which contain in them very startling reve-
lations of Divine truth. It is a saying of
Divine truth in which we are all individually
concerned. It reaches to the very least of us.
In it we may all learn to see our superior blessing, and at the same time our greater responsibility.

For if you rightly understand it, brethren,
the LORD JESUS here tells you, even the least

of you, that you are *greater than S. John the Baptist*. Let us then endeavour to understand this saying of our LORD's.

On the Day of Pentecost the LORD, the HOLY GHOST, came down from Heaven, and through the ministry of the Apostles began the new dispensation of Grace. He opened the Kingdom of CHRIST upon earth. Then that Kingdom of Heaven began upon earth of which the Baptist had given clear warning, saying, " The Kingdom of Heaven is at hand."

And that Kingdom has remained here ever since. We have entered into it by the same door by which the first believers entered on the Day of Pentecost, namely, in our Baptism; for this is the one only door of entrance into His New Kingdom, which the LORD, the King Himself, has made. For no words of His are more express or more absolute than these : " Verily, verily, I say unto thee, Except a man be born of water and of the Spirit, he cannot enter into the kingdom of GOD."

Now, therefore, let us consider what our LORD says concerning the state of those who have entered into this new Kingdom of GOD : " Verily I say unto you, Among them that are born of women, there hath not risen a greater than John the Baptist: notwithstanding, he that is least in the Kingdom of Heaven is greater than he."

S. John the Baptist, our LORD declares, was greater than any saint or prophet of former ages. This need not so much mean that he was greater in respect of personal holiness, or zeal, or faith, as that he was greater in respect of his office and ministry. For the prophets of former ages only prophesied of the coming of the LORD as a distant future event. S. John did more than this, for he announced the actual Advent of GOD Incarnate; he pointed out to the people the actual presence of the LORD, saying, " Behold the Lamb of GOD !"

Moses was great in his day, but he only introduced the Jewish dispensation, a dispensation full of types and shadows, all of them only foreshadowing what was to come at some distant day. But the Baptist proclaimed the Kingdom of the LORD as close at hand.

Isaiah was great in his day, but he saw the glory of the LORD only afar off. S. John beheld Him face to face. Isaiah prophesied, saying of the Messiah, " The Spirit of the LORD shall rest upon Him," but the Baptist actually baptized the LORD JESUS, and so was instrumental in fulfilling that very prophecy, and in constituting Him the very CHRIST.

So that it is plain that in his office, in his

privileges, in his ministry, S. John was "more than a prophet;" he had more honour and higher blessing given him than any saint before him, as the immediate forerunner of GOD Incarnate.

Not one of the former believers in GOD had ever been so great in spiritual gifts and blessings as S. John the Baptist, "Notwithstanding (our LORD says) he that is least in the Kingdom of Heaven is greater than he." The least officer, the least minister, yea, even the least member, in the Kingdom of Heaven, the new Kingdom of GOD Incarnate, is greater than the Baptist.

This then, you see, brethren, belongs to you and to me. Here is a Divine truth which concerns us every one, even the very least member of the Church of CHRIST.

If we have been entered into this Kingdom of Heaven in our second birth by water and the HOLY GHOST, then is our spiritual condition a condition of greater privilege, of greater grace, of greater blessing, than the condition of John the Baptist or of any of the saints before him.

For the Baptist himself did not actually enter into this Kingdom of Heaven upon earth. He was cut off by wicked Herod's sword before the Kingdom of CHRIST was set up. He only

E

said "The Kingdom of Heaven is at hand," but he did not live to see its actual advent. He did not himself enter into it.

But we have entered into it. We are now living in it. All its mysteries are now revealed unto us. All its grace and all its truth are come unto us. So that the least amongst us, our LORD tells us, is greater in spiritual gifts and blessings than any of the saints of elder dispensations.

Now we might almost have thought that it would be so, of our own selves. Because how could it be possible that the Advent of GOD in the flesh should not bring us greater blessings than any ever before given to man? Surely the presence of the Kingdom of the Incarnate LORD amongst us must confer upon us gifts and blessings superior to all that were ever granted before.

It is sufficient to show us the truth of this, if we now call to mind those special gifts of Grace which are given us by our LORD's own institution in the two great Sacraments of the Gospel dispensation.

In the first, what is the special grace, what is the distinguishing gift, given even to the very least of us? To sum up all in one word, we are made, in our baptism, by the power of the HOLY GHOST, "members of CHRIST." This is the distinctive gift of Christian Baptism. We are made members of the Second Adam, members of a new Divine Life-giving Head, members of the new Head of the human family, members of the Incarnate Word.

Now this, our regeneration in CHRIST, is a new gift of Divine grace. This membership with the Second Adam is a gift of Grace which none of the saints of the former dispensations ever had, or even could have had, before the LORD Himself was incarnate.

As members of the Second Adam, therefore, the very least of us possesses a gift of Grace greater than any of the elder saints ever possessed.

Then call to mind the special gift of the other great Sacrament of CHRIST. S. Paul teaches us this, saying, "The Bread which we break, is it not the communion of the Body of CHRIST? The Cup of blessing which we bless, is it not the Communion of the Blood of CHRIST?"

Here it is plain, again, that none of the elder saints could ever have received these Divine gifts—gifts of Grace which were waiting for their communication until the eternal LORD had been made man. None of them ever received, or could have received, this Holy Communion of the Body and Blood of GOD Incarnate; by means of which Divine Gifts that indwelling Presence of GOD is now granted to us which was so often spoken of in old time, when it was promised, "I will dwell in them and walk in them."

It was not until our LORD had given to His Disciples this Holy Communion that He spoke to them of this His own indwelling presence. And to this higher indwelling Divine Presence our LORD also plainly referred when He said of the coming of the HOLY GHOST, " He dwelleth with you, and shall be in you."

And then also to speak for a moment, brethren, of the sacred offices of the Christian Ministry.   We now hold an office in the Kingdom of CHRIST far greater in spiritual dignity, grace, and power, than any that any prophet, priest, or king ever held, before the Advent of the LORD GOD incarnate.   For it belongs to the spiritual power of the office which we now hold to baptize you into the Kingdom of Heaven; to declare and pronounce to you, on your repentance and faith, the absolution and remission of your sins; and to break that Bread which is the Communion of the Body of CHRIST, and to bless that Cup, which is the Communion of His Blood.

S. John the Baptist could not have done any one of these things.

But let us all learn one other lesson from

this saying of the Son of God. If we now
possess, even the very least of us, a condition
of greater blessing, and privilege, and grace,
than that of any of the saints in former dispensations, then it must certainly follow that
our responsibilities are greater also.

To whom God gives His best gifts, of them
also He justly expects the most and the best
fruits. We ought therefore, and we might, excel
all the saints of the former ages in the fruits of
repentance and faith, of love and zeal. In the
Day of Judgment *we* must be judged by the
highest standard of all.

Are you not, then, brethren, almost ready
to wish that you had been born before the
Advent of the Lord from Heaven? Are you
not almost ready to wish that you had never
been entered into the Kingdom of Heaven?
Have you any just sense of this your greater
responsibility? Are you giving all diligence
to walk " worthy of the Lord unto all pleasing?" Are you so using the means of Grace
now appointed for you, that you are growing
up in all things into Him Who is the Head?
Are you striving to attain unto the fulness of
the stature of the perfect Man, even to walk
before God " as becometh saints," even saints
of the Christian dispensation, walking even as
He walked?

SERMON VII.

THE SECOND MAN.

𝔗𝔥𝔦𝔯𝔡 𝔖𝔲𝔫𝔡𝔞𝔶 𝔦𝔫 𝔄𝔡𝔳𝔢𝔫𝔱.

1 Cor. xv. 47.

"The Second Man is the Lord from Heaven."

You all know, brethren, who is meant in these words. It is the Person of our Lord and Saviour Jesus Christ. He is "the Lord from Heaven;" and, He is "the Second Man."

Let us consider this description of our Saviour's twofold Nature.

1. Our Saviour is "the Lord from Heaven." He did not begin to be, when He came into this world. But He came down "from Heaven." In Heaven He had been from the beginning with God; in Heaven He had been in the glory of the Father, before the worlds began to be created; God of God, Light of

Light, Very GOD of Very GOD; the SON of
GOD by an eternal generation; being of one
Substance with the FATHER.

No Angel, brethren, no Archangel, is our
SAVIOUR. But He is the LORD Himself, who
could say of Himself without any blasphemy,
"I AM;" "I and My FATHER are One;"
"He that hath seen Me, hath seen the FA-
THER." He is, as S. Paul writes, "GOD our
SAVIOUR."

2. But He is also now made "the Second
Man." This is the profound Mystery of the
Incarnation. "Great is the Mystery of god-
liness," writes S. Paul, "GOD manifest in the
flesh." And S. John writes, "In the begin-
ning was the Word, and the Word was with
GOD, and the Word was GOD." And "the
Word was made Flesh, and dwelt among us."

By virtue of His Divine Nature, then, brethren, all the attributes and perfections of the
Eternal Godhead, and, by virtue of His Human
Nature, all the perfections of the Manhood, are
possessed by our SAVIOUR. Here is the Mystery
of all Mysteries; the Godhead and the Manhood now for ever united together in one
Person, the Person of our SAVIOUR, GOD the
SON, made Man.

3. What question then, brethren, do we all
naturally wish to ask, as soon as we have this

great Mystery declared unto us? It must be this; "Why is God thus made Man?"

One answer to this question is at once, "That He might be our SAVIOUR." But then we naturally ask, "Why should it be necessary that God should be made Man in order to be our SAVIOUR? Why could not God save us simply as God, without taking upon Himself our human nature?"

Now there are many answers to this great question. It will be quite sufficient for us on the present occasion if we try to understand *one* of these answers.

Let me endeavour to explain to you one great answer to the great question, "Why was God made Man?" It is an answer which is drawn from the title given to our SAVIOUR in our text, "The Second Man."

4. Let us try to understand this. It is written that "the works of God are double, one against another." The lower works of God in nature often correspond with His higher works in grace. Our first creation in Adam bears a wonderful resemblance to our second creation in CHRIST. Adam, the First Man, S. Paul expressly writes, is "a figure of Him that was to come," i.e. of CHRIST, the Second Adam.

Let us then consider one or two of the chief

respects in which the First Man and the Second Man bear this likeness one to the other; for this will greatly help us to understand why our SAVIOUR is called "the Second Man."

The First Man, Adam, then, was so constituted by GOD that he should be the head and source of life to the whole human family.

GOD poured out upon the First Man many excellent gifts. He made his nature to be in many respects, and in certain degrees, a true likeness or image of His own Divine Nature.

And this Nature was not to remain alone in the First Man. It was to be communicated from him to all the family of mankind.

GOD might have created each individual man by himself alone, just as He created the First Man.

But it is not so. GOD creates no one independently of the First Man. We have all received our being from the First Man. We have all received our human life and our human nature from the one head of the human family, the First Man. His nature, both in body and soul, has been communicated to each one of us. Our bodily life has been derived to us, by a marvellous succession, from his bodily life. We are, individually, "members of his body, from his flesh and from his bones."

And not only so, brethren. In another re-

spect we all inherit and receive from the First
Man his condition as a fallen creature; we inherit from him a spiritual condition tainted with
evil.   The son is born into the same condition
into which his father fell by sin.   We have all
inherited from the first Adam "a body of sin
and death."   As S. Paul writes, "By one man's
disobedience, the many were made sinners."

5. Now, then, let us consider.   Here is GOD's
amazing plan for our restoration and salvation.
A Second Man is constituted.   A New Head
and Source of Life is given to mankind.   A
Second Adam is born into our human family.
The LORD from Heaven, the Eternal SON of
GOD, comes down from Heaven, and is made
the Second Man.

In His Person all the original perfections of
the Manhood are restored.   He is made Man,
in all the excellencies of the human nature.

His Life began upon earth in exceeding great
humility.   It was one life-long Sacrifice for us.
But having fulfilled all righteousness, having
been obedient unto the will of the FATHER
from the first, all along, every day and every
hour, in every thought, in every word, and in
every deed, even unto the Death of the Cross;
having been made perfect through suffering;
having, by His Sacrifice of Himself, obtained
eternal redemption for us; having risen from

the dead, He ascended into Heaven. There
GOD the FATHER hath most highly exalted Him,
and given Him to be Head over all things to
the Church.

There therefore we now see Him, in power
and glory supreme. There is now the Second
Man, even in the glory of the FATHER. Now
therefore we may change the words of our text
a little, and say,—The Second Man is the LORD
in Heaven; the Second Man reigns in glory,
on the Throne of the FATHER.

And now, brethren, let us consider the relationship in which we stand to Him Who is thus
made in our nature, Who is thus the LORD Incarnate. His Title, the Second Adam, teaches
us at once that He is the Second Head of the
human family. He has been made the Second
Man for the very end that we might be made
members of Him. For how could we be made
members of the SON of GOD simply as He is
GOD?

By His Incarnation it is that GOD the SON has
been made the True Vine, in order that we might
be grafted in upon Him, and so receive life of
His Life. As the Second Man it is that our
SAVIOUR is our New Divine Life-giving Head,
communicating to His members of His own
Life, making them partakers of His own restored and perfect Manhood.

This Manhood is now in the Incarnate LORD *for our participation,* in order that through our union and membership with Him we may receive again a perfect and an immortal Manhood.

Our fallen, sinful, perishing humanity, brethren, is to be cleansed, healed, restored, and glorified, only by union and communion with the Divine Humanity of the Second Man, the Incarnate Word. It is only as we are in Him that we are made partakers of His Life and of His Righteousness. We are saved, let us understand, only through union with our Divine Head, the Second Adam.

Good feelings, pious hopes and wishes, repentance, faith, holiness, prayers,—none of these things save us; none of these things, however good and however necessary they are, give us Life; none of these things save us. Our Eternal Life, our Saving Grace, is alone in CHRIST, and comes to us through our union with Him.

Do you ask the great question, then, brethren, Why is the SON of GOD made Man? why was that great and marvellous mystery necessary for our salvation? One answer is plainly this, —It is, in order that He may be unto us a New Life-Giving Head, so that, as we all receive our natural life from the First Man, we

may receive our new Eternal Life from the
Second Man; as we all receive our fallen manhood from the fallen manhood of the First
Man, we may receive a restored, perfect, sinless, immortal Manhood, from the Divine Manhood of the Second Man; as we all receive a
fallen condition, "a body of sin and death,"
from the First Man, we .may receive a glorious
body from the Second Man, a body fashioned
like unto His glorious Body, sinless and death-
less for ever.

6. For the analogy is perfect. Our first natural creation in Adam is a perfect foreshadowing of our second creation in CHRIST. In the
lower creation we are literally, "Members of the
body of the First Man, from his flesh and from
his bones." In the New Creation we are, as
really and as truly, members of the Body of
the Second Man. For S. Paul expressly so ap-
plies the words, "We are members of His Body,
from His flesh and from His bones," (Eph. v.
30,) in a passage where he is particularly com-
paring our first creation in Adam and Eve to
·our new creation in CHRIST and His Church.

7. Thus, then, brethren, one essential part of
our Christian faith is this, that if we live in
union with CHRIST, our Life-giving Head, "the
Second Man," and if we die in union with
Him, then is our hope full of glory and immor-

tality; then we shall be raised up at last in
Him; made partakers of that glorious perfect
Manhood which is in Him, each one of us in some
likeness to Him; that as we now bear some
likeness of the First Man, so then we shall each
bear some likeness of the heavenly Adam, the
Second Man.

For then the little seed now sown within us
will bear its glorious fruit; then the little germ
of life, now planted within us at our Baptism
into CHRIST, and now nourished within us by
the Holy Communion of His living and Life-
giving Body and Blood, will be developed into
the glorious likeness of the Second Man, the
Incarnate SON of GOD.

8. In conclusion, brethren, let me say ;—first
of all, see the Divine plan of Eternal Wisdom, for
the restoration, the regeneration, the salvation
of the fallen family of the First Man.   It is by
means of the Second Man.   It is through the
profound Mystery of the Incarnation of the
Eternal Word.   It is through the Advent of
the SON of GOD into our human family.

See next, brethren, our grand glory.   The
Second Man, our new Head, is the very LORD
from Heaven, now reigning in Heaven in the
glory of the FATHER.   Now our life is hid with
CHRIST in GOD; but when He shall appear
again, we shall also appear with Him in glory

everlasting. Then all that we lost in the First Man will be restored, and more than restored in the Second.

Consider thirdly, brethren, that all our hope, all our salvation, all our life, all our glory, all depends, most essentially, upon our union with the Second Man, our Divine Life-giving Head.

This union, brethren, is no mere figure of speech; it is no mere sentiment; it is something real and actual; a present gift of grace within us. Our union with CHRIST, the Second Adam, is as true and as real a thing as our union with the First Adam. It is not CHRIST at a distance who is our Life; no, it is CHRIST *in us*, which alone is our Life and our Salvation. We must be made one with CHRIST, and CHRIST with us. There must be a union between us and the Second Adam, as true and as real as between us and the First.

It is plain, brethren, that we ourselves can no more cause or make this union than we could at first create our own selves. It is beyond the power of man; it is beyond the power of nature. It is the gift of the grace and of the power of GOD alone, through the HOLY GHOST.

GOD therefore of His infinite goodness has Himself ordained for us the means of obtaining this union with the Second Man. CHRIST

Himself has instituted for us in His Church two great Sacraments of the Gospel, as the appointed channels through which He conveys to us those gifts of His Grace which are necessary to give us, and to sustain in us, this membership and union with Himself.

In the first Sacrament, the Sacrament of our Regeneration, we are made members of CHRIST, members of the Second Adam. Our union with our New Divine Head is then begun, through the Power of the HOLY GHOST.

In the other Sacrament the LORD grants us His own indwelling Presence, from time to time, through the Holy Communion of His Living and Life-giving Body and Blood; so that, from time to time, (if we receive these Heavenly Gifts in true repentance and obedient faith,) we are made one with CHRIST and CHRIST with us. Our union with our Divine Head is sustained in us.

Hence it is, brethren, you will easily understand, that our LORD has made these two Sacraments necessary for your salvation, if you desire to be saved by Him.

Lastly, brethren, prepare, I beseech you, to celebrate the Human Birthday of the LORD from Heaven with all the reverence and devotion in your power. Never think that you have ever yet kept the LORD's Birthday as you ought to have done. The joy of the Nativity of the SON of GOD in our human family has never yet filled your heart as it ought.

Especially, I beseech you, prepare to worship GOD, on His SON's Human Birthday, with that one special Act of worship which is instituted and commanded by the LORD Himself; in which also He comes to give Himself to us, *so* as He does at no other time, and in no other way, even to all who seek Him as the only Hope, the only Strength, the only Light of Life, the only Glory of our being.

To Whom, once for us lying in the manger, now reigning in the glory of the FATHER, be humbly ascribed, by men and angels, all supremest honour and glory, for ever and ever. Amen.

SERMON VIII.

___

OUR ELDER BROTHER.

Third Sunday in Advent.

ROMANS VIII. 29.

"THAT HE MIGHT BE THE FIRST-BORN AMONG MANY
BRETHREN."

WHAT, brethren, do you think, is the grand
glory of our human race? Perhaps you will
say, our grand glory is that we were created in
the image and likeness of our great Creator.

This was indeed an exceedingly grand glory.
But, brethren, do we not all know and feel
how miserably that glory has been spoilt and
lost through sin? GOD, therefore, most merciful and gracious, foreseeing this our loss and
ruin, in the riches of His grace, fore-ordained
for us a still greater glory.

What, brethren, is this greater glory? What
is now our grand glory; a glory far beyond

the glory of our first creation? It is this: that He Who created all things, even the Second Person in the ever-living and all-glorious Godhead, He Who at first created man in His own Image, should be Himself now made in our image. It is this: that He Who is GOD and LORD of all, should be Himself now made Man. It is this: that He Who is the Eternal SON of the FATHER, should be born into our human family, and made the Son of Mary. In one word: our grand glory is this, that GOD is manifest in our human nature in the Second Person of the Godhead, as S. Paul writes, "Great is the mystery of godliness, GOD manifest in the flesh."

If you had never heard of this profound mystery before, brethren, you would hardly be able to believe it. You would be ready to take up your hats and walk out of Church at hearing me tell you such a cunningly devised fable. For this is indeed the mystery of all mysteries, the miracle of all miracles, that the Eternal SON of GOD should be born into our human family, and made the Son of the Blessed Virgin.

Every Advent Season, brethren, you should endeavour to have your faith increased in this profound mystery of godliness, this Foundation of our religion, even GOD made Man, our grand glory.

For Advent Season is appointed by the Church, brethren, in order that in it our hearts and minds may be, in some degree, more prepared to celebrate the human Birthday of the LORD from Heaven; when He Who was in the glory of the FATHER, was openly revealed to our mortal sight here below; made the Son of Mary, laid down in the lowly manger, born into our common human family, made one with us.

For this, brethren, is the mighty salvation which GOD has raised up for us, in the house of His servant David. This is the very thing that GOD fore-ordained for us from all eternity, that for our salvation, His own well-beloved and co-equal SON should be made our very Brother; so that He should become, by His Incarnation and His Nativity in our family, as it is expressed in the words of our text, the First-born, the Elder One, among many brethren.

For must we not believe at once, that if He is born into our family, Who is GOD and LORD of all, He must bring with Him into our human family the very riches of Heaven? He must bring with Him all that we can possibly need, to relieve us of all our miseries, to redeem us from our captivity to sin and death, to cleanse, to heal, to restore, to save, to bless, to glorify us for ever. It is one of our Proverbs, that " a brother is born for adversity." If He therefore is made the First-born, the Elder Brother among many brethren, even He Who is the LORD from Heaven, then must we not be very sure, that He brings with Him into our family perfect remedies for all our adversity; He comes to bring us a mighty salvation from all evil, and a most glorious exaltation to eternal life?

And here, brethren, to help you to feel all the more deeply how very much is necessarily implied in this Title of our LORD, " the Firstborn among many brethren," let me remind you of the history, which is written in 1 Kings xx.

Benhadad, king of Syria, fought against the king of Israel with all his hosts. But the Israelites prevailed against the Syrians, and slew them with a very great slaughter. Benhadad fled away for his life, and hid himself.

"Then his servants came to him and said to him, Behold now, we have heard that the kings of the house of Israel are merciful kings; let us, I pray thee, put sackcloth on our loins, and ropes upon our heads, and go out to the king of Israel, peradventure he will save thy life.

" So they girded sackcloth on their loins, and put ropes on their heads, and came to the king of Israel, and said, Thy servant Benhadad

saith, I pray thee let me live. And he said, Is
he yet alive? He is my brother.

"Now the men did diligently observe
whether any thing would come from him, and
did hastily catch it; and they said, Thy brother
Benhadad. Then he said, Go ye, bring him.
Then Benhadad came forth to him, and he
caused him to come up into the chariot."

Those Syrians, who had fought with all their
might against the king of Israel, justly expected nothing but death. So they very
anxiously observed what the king of Israel
should say to their petition. And when he
used the word "brother," when he said, "Is
he yet alive? he is my brother," then did they
hastily catch that word. That one word re-
vived their fainting hearts, and saved them at
once from despair; that one word they hastily
caught, and laid hold of, and repeated, and
said, "Thy brother, Benhadad."

It saved them from all their miserable
fears, it filled their hearts at once with joyful hope.

And soon the brother was brought forth
from his hiding-place, and soon the merciful
king of Israel forgave the brother who had
fought against him, and not only forgave, but
caused him to come up and sit with himself,
even in his own chariot.

I think, brethren, I need not interpret the history. You will all easily see through it.

We are the wicked Syrians who have fought with all our might against the true King of Israel. But He is a merciful King, ready to forgive every penitent sinner who prays for His mercy.

For He has, indeed, made Himself our very and true Brother. He has taken upon Himself our very nature; not the nature of angels, but the nature of man; so that we are now indeed related to the LORD as no other created beings are; "He is the First-born among many brethren."

And when He had laid down His human life for our sins, and when He had risen from the dead, let us diligently observe whether any word comes from Him; let us mark with great care and anxiety His first words. And what is His first sentence? Is it, " Go, tell those My cruel enemies, who killed Me?" Is it, "Go, tell My disciples, those base cowards, who all forsook Me in the time of danger?"

No. What are the words? "Go to My brethren, and say unto them, I ascend unto My FATHER and your FATHER, and to My GOD and your GOD."

Shall we not then hastily catch that word? Shall we not treasure it up in our hearts?

Shall we not repeat it to ourselves over and over again, " Go to My brethren ?"

Behold the very and true King of Glory has made Himself as one of us ! Behold He Who is one with the FATHER is not ashamed then to call us " brethren."

He " is the First-born among many brethren." Before the Nativity of the LORD we were only creatures of His hand. But now what are we ? He Himself says, " Go to My brethren."

Now, therefore, we have a nearness to the living GOD, a relationship to the LORD of all, which is not granted to any other creature. You may by faith, brethren, look up into the highest Heaven, and there you may see One, in the very glory of the FATHER, made like unto us ; One in our human nature, our true Elder Brother, our new Divine Head ; the Second Adam, the New Man, the LORD JESUS, our LORD and our GOD ; perfect GOD and perfect Man.

Here then is our grand eternal glory, GOD the SON made Man, the very LORD from Heaven made the Second Man, the eternal SON of GOD made the Son of Mary, in order to be our Salvation, our Life, our Joy, our grand eternal Glory.

Oh let us, then, for ever praise the infinite

Love of God in ordaining for us from eternal ages this mighty Salvation. Let us praise God, this Advent Season, for the clear open revelation of this inexpressibly great and glorious mystery, falling down before that lowly throne in the cattle-stall at Bethlehem, and worshipping Him Whom the heaven of heavens cannot contain, "lying in the manger," in exceeding great humility, past all our thoughts.

And before He comes down from Heaven in all His divine power and glory, oh let us learn to believe in Him, to trust in Him, to keep His words, to venture everything on His words, to follow Him, to yield up ourselves unto Him in truth and sincerity, so that in that day when we shall see Him as He is, we may not be ashamed before Him at His coming.

One saying of our Lord's, brethren, let us consider a moment in conclusion. One day, " whilst He was talking to the people, behold His Mother and His brethren stood without desiring to speak to Him. Then one said unto Him, Behold Thy Mother and Thy brethren stand without desiring to speak with Thee. And He stretched forth His hand towards His disciples, and said, Behold My Mother and My brethren! For whosoever shall do the will of My Father which is in Heaven, the same is My brother, and sister, and mother."

Let us all, then, judge our own selves, brethren, by this saying of our LORD's.   Because
it is most sure, that a certain character must
be formed within us before ever we shall be
able, or permitted, to behold Him Who is our
Divine Brother in all His majesty in peace.

We must be conformed to the image of the
SON of GOD, in the spirit of our minds, before
we can be admitted into His presence, and
taken up into the throne of His glory.

And what is the most essential feature of
this character?   Our LORD Himself here
marks it—"Whosoever shall do the will of
My FATHER which is in Heaven."   For concerning the whole of His own life on earth,
He said, "My meat is to do the will of Him
that sent Me, and to finish His work."

Even so, brethren, the same mind should be
formed within us which was in Him.   And
therefore we pray to GOD always at every
Evening Service, that "our hearts may be set
to obey His commandments."

But here, brethren, is our daily trial.   Here,
of course, we all have our daily hindrances,
our various difficulties, our several temptations.
But "hereby do we know that we know Him
(writes S. John) if we keep His commandments."

Is it, then, brethren, your daily meat and

drink, in some true degree, to do the will of GOD; to submit your own will to His; to seek in all things to please GOD, Who seeth in secret, Who trieth the hearts? Are you giving all diligence to keep the precepts of the Gospel? Are you observing the sayings of the SON of GOD? Are you venturing your all on His words?

"The world passeth away and the lust thereof, but he that doeth the will of GOD abideth for ever."

SERMON IX.

THE BEGINNING OF THE NEW CREATION.

Third Sunday in Advent.

REV. IV. 4.

"THE BEGINNING OF THE CREATION OF GOD."

LET us consider what is necessarily implied in this Divine title, by which our SAVIOUR revealed Himself to the Church of Laodicea; by which also He still reveals Himself to us.

First, it is plain, our LORD is so called, because He is Himself the Creator of all things. For S. John writes, "All things were made by Him, and without Him was not anything made that was made."

And S. Paul writes, "Who is the Image of the invisible GOD, the First-born of every creature; for by Him were all things created that are in heaven and that are in earth, visible and invisible, whether they be thrones, or dominions, or principalities, or powers; all things were created by Him and for Him, and He is before all things, and by Him all things consist."

And again, " His Son, Whom He hath appointed Heir of all things, by Whom also He made the worlds."

And so the Church confesses in the Nicene Creed, " God of God, Light of Light, very God of very God, of one Substance with the Father, by Whom all things were made."

From all which passages we learn, that the eternal Son of God, the everlasting Word, is He by Whom all the worlds of the universe were created. It is He by Whom the Father spake and it was done, by Whom He commanded and it stood fast; by Whom He said, " Let there be light, and there was light."

Our Lord, therefore, is thus " the Beginning of the creation of God," the First producing Cause of the whole creation; moulding all things according to the will of His own eternal wisdom ; giving to each world its own laws and excellences, fashioning every plant, and every animal, and every intelligent being, in their several kinds, and giving them all their respective perfections, according to His own good pleasure.

Moreover, we learn, that it is in Him that the whole creation still consists, moment by moment, being upheld by the incessant working of His Divine power. All creation is, therefore, an open and visible revelation of the eternal and Divine LORD. As S. Paul writes: "The invisible things of Him from the creation of the world are clearly seen." (Rom. i. 20.) Manifold mysteries of His wisdom, of His goodness, and of His power, are shown forth, in various measures, in all His creatures.

All orders of being, visible and invisible, have their life in Him. He is the life of all. He is the sustaining Power of all. "In Him we live, and move, and have our being." This is the first sense of this Divine title of the Son of GOD, "The Beginning of the Creation of GOD."

II. Next, the eternal SON is the Beginning of the Creation of GOD forasmuch as He is Himself, as made Man, the First Cause and Power of our regeneration, i.e., of our new creation.

When this world had fallen from GOD, and was at enmity with GOD, and was sinking into eternal ruin, then the same Divine Power of endless life, out of which, in the beginning, we first derived our life and being, became to us a power of restoration and regeneration. When we had fallen, through sin, from GOD, the voice was heard in prophecy, " Behold I make all things new."

During the first 4000 years of the world the SON of GOD was preparing all things for the great mystery of this new creation, until the fulness of time should come, when He, the Word Himself, should be made Flesh and should dwell among us, full of grace and truth. Then was the first actual beginning of the new creation. By the unspeakable mystery of the Divine Incarnation, a New Creation began in Him. The Eternal Word made flesh, is " the Beginning." He, the LORD from Heaven, is the Second Man.

Our manhood, which through the fall of the first man was spoiled, the Eternal LORD Himself took, in all its original perfections; He was made perfect Man. He lived in our manhood, through all its stages, in childhood, youth, and age. He hallowed it, He filled it with the Divine Presence, and restored it to GOD. In our manhood He died, and He raised it from the dead, and then He exalted it above the conditions of matter and sense. Of a natural body He made a spiritual body, and this, on His Ascension, He carried up to the highest glory, and presented it at the right hand of GOD.

There the Eternal SON of GOD Incarnate now ever lives, perfect Man as well as perfect GOD. There, O most amazing truth, most stupendous mystery, our manhood is exalted above all the creation of GOD, being for ever united to the Godhead in the person of the Eternal Word.

Now the New Adam, the Second Man, is arrayed in Divine glory, at the right hand of the Majesty on high.

Such is the infinite mystery of the Incarnation as now fulfilled in the Kingdom of GOD. The mystery was only beginning during our LORD's life on earth, now it is fulfilled by His Resurrection from the dead, and by His Ascension into the Heaven of Heavens in our manhood. Now our manhood is restored unto GOD. In the Divine manhood of the Eternal LORD most high, at GOD's right hand, is the restoration of this creation of GOD.

For for us, brethren, has this infinite mystery been fulfilled, and for our salvation. To this purpose of the Divine Incarnation let us now confine our thoughts.

III. Let us now consider how our own eternal life and glory is contained in this mystery of the Incarnation of the SON of GOD.

Just as the first creation was not one single act, but a sustained and continuous act, so also is the second creation. The power of that primeval benediction, "Be fruitful and multiply," is continuous. It has the same force now as at the beginning. The first man was not made for himself only, but in order to be the beginning, the head, the spring of life and being, to a whole family.

Even so the Second Man was made to be the New Source of life, the Head of a new family, the Beginning of a new creation. At our second birth we are created anew in CHRIST JESUS. As members of the Second Man we receive a new beginning of life. We receive life from His life. He becomes our New Divine Life-giving Head.

A new family of man is thus created, which is the mystical body of the Eternal SON. He is the Second Adam, our new Divine Head. Whatever the first Adam is to us, according to the flesh and according to nature, that is the Second Adam to us, according to the Spirit and according to Grace.

By nature we are one with the first Adam, the father of all flesh; we are partakers of his manhood, members of his body, bone of his bone, flesh of his flesh. In the kingdom of Grace, the new creation, we are one with the Second Adam, partakers of His Divine Manhood, members of His Body, bone of His bone,

and flesh of His flesh. By our membership
with the first father of mankind, we receive our
natural life, with its various capacities; so by
our membership with the Second Head of mankind we receive our spiritual life, with all its
capacities of eternal glory.

We are made, through union with the Eternal Son Incarnate, partakers of that Manhood
which is in Him, sinless, perfect, and immortal;
we are incorporated into that Body, of which
the Second Adam is the Head, the Life, and
the Beginning,—we enter into the new Creation of God.

Thus, in the infinite Mystery of the Incarnation of the Eternal Word, is contained the
glorious Mystery of our own perfect restoration,
in body, soul, and spirit. Thus by the Advent
of God in the flesh have all things been made
new. Thus is God the Son, being made Man,
the Beginning of a New Creation.

Consider, brethren, how S. Paul expressly
declares this Mystery to us in his Epistle to
the Colossians; passing on from the old to the
new Creation.

" Who is the Image of the invisible God;
the First-born of every creature; for by Him
were all things created, that are in heaven, and
that are in earth, visible and invisible, whether
they be thrones, or dominions, or principalities,

or powers; all things were created by Him, and for Him; and He is before all things; and by Him all things consist."

Here is the First Creation,—the whole of it by Him, and for Him, and in Him.

Then the Apostle goes on to the Second Creation, saying: "And He is the Head of the Body, the Church; Who is the Beginning, the First-born from the dead, that in all things He might have the pre-eminence. For it pleased the FATHER that in Him should all fulness dwell."

Just as Eve, the mother of all living, was a second creation, but created out of the body of the first Adam, so it is with the Church, which is the Bride of CHRIST, formed out of the Body of the Second Adam, created to be one with Himself for ever,—His Mystical Body.

Our Regeneration, that is our New Creation, consists in being made members of the Mystical Body of the Second Adam. Then He becomes our New Divine Life-giving Head. Then we enter into the New Creation, as it is expressly written, "If any man be in CHRIST, he is a new creation." And again, "We are His workmanship [that is a second time] created in CHRIST JESUS."

For here we should distinctly consider that, this our union in one body with the Incarnate

SON of GOD, our New Divine Head, is a distinct Divine gift. It is not merely a union of will or of feeling, it does not consist in any acts of repentance, faith, or love; it is a distinct gift, given to us by the power of the HOLY GHOST.

Let us also consider that, as far as we are able to know, this Incarnation of the SON of GOD was necessary in order that we might be united to Him as our Divine Head. For it would seem impossible that we could be united to the Godhead directly. At any rate, so it has been ordained to be, that the Eternal Word should Himself be Incarnate, and that so we should be united to His Manhood, and so to the Eternal Godhead.

By the infinite Mystery of an eternal generation, the SON Himself is of one substance with the FATHER, and, as He said of Himself, He lives by the FATHER. And now, by the infinite Mystery of the Incarnation, He is become of one substance with us. He is consubstantial, therefore, both with the FATHER and with us. Both the Godhead and the Manhood exist in Him in all fulness of power and perfection.

And then by another infinite Mystery, as the SON Himself lives, by being of one substance with the FATHER, so we now live by the SON, by partaking of His substance, by being made one with Him. As He Himself teaches

us : "As the FATHER hath life in Himself, so
hath He given to the SON to have life in Himself;" and moreover, "As the Living FATHER
hath sent Me, and I live by the FATHER; so
he that eateth Me, even he shall live by Me;"
because it is through the Holy Communion
of His Living and Life-giving Body and Blood
that we are now sustained in union with our
Divine Head, and receive continual supplies
of life from His life.

For as the Union of the FATHER and the
SON is no figure of speech, but a most real and
true Union in one substance, so our union with
the Eternal SON made Flesh is not any figure
of speech, but a most true and real union in
one substance.

"For both He that sanctifieth, and they
who are sanctified are all of one; for which
cause He is not ashamed to call them brethren."
(Heb. ii. 11.)   Both He and we, the Apostle
says, are "of one," that is, of one FATHER, or
of one nature, or of one substance.

As the SON partakes of the Godhead of the
FATHER, so we partake of the Manhood of the
SON ; as He lives by the FATHER, so we live
by Him.   He is our Life and our Quickening
Spirit.

So that if we preserve our union with the
Incarnate SON, if we live and die "in CHRIST,"

then all the perfections of our restored manhood will be revealed and developed in us, in body, soul, and spirit, in the glories of eternity; each of us bearing some likeness to the Second Adam, our Divine Head, "the Beginning of the Creation of God," "the Head of the Body, the Church."

For in that day of all days which is coming, at His Second Advent, the Lord Incarnate, the Second Man, will present unto Himself the New Creation, the True Eve, His Mystical Body, His Bride for whom He gave Himself, cleansed from every defilement, healed, restored, and glorified, to be one with Himself for ever.

What manner of persons then, brethren, ought we to be, hastening unto this day of God? How should we be putting on more and more of the New Man every day, that we may be found in Him, and be prepared for that open revelation of His glory, when He will present unto Himself every true and faithful disciple.

SERMON X.

OUR NEW GIFTS.

Third Sunday in Advent.

S. John i. 17.

"The Law was given by Moses: but Grace and
Truth came by Jesus Christ."

These words do not mean, brethren, that no
measures of Grace, and that no portions of
Truth were ever granted before the coming of
our Lord. But they do plainly and emphati-
cally mean that the grace and the truth which
were given in former ages were given in very
far less measures than they are now. They do
mean that the former gifts are not worthy to
be compared with that Grace and that Truth
which are now revealed and given unto us in
the Church of Christ.

Before the sun rises we are thankful for star-
light, but when the sun is risen we no more
remember the light of the stars.

Before the LORD came all was in comparative darkness. But when the Eternal LORD was made flesh and dwelt among us; when the SON of GOD was born into our human family; when " that Eternal Life which was with the FATHER was manifested unto us;" when "the LORD from Heaven" was made "the Second Man ;" to be the new life and head of the human race, "full of grace and truth," then the true Sun of Glory arose upon us, then that voice of the Prophet was fulfilled, "Arise, shine, for thy Light is come, and the glory of the LORD is risen upon thee." Then came the full dispensation of the grace and of the truth of GOD.

Before the Advent of GOD in the flesh, some degrees of truth were revealed, and some measures of grace were given. GOD gave many promises and covenants; He ordained many types, and figures, and shadows, and services; all of them rather prefiguring, than actually giving, the good things that were promised.

The Law was given by Moses, holy, just, and good; but it was only " a schoolmaster to bring us to CHRIST." But when the LORD, the Messiah, the CHRIST Himself came, then all was changed into reality and substance; the water of the Jewish dispensation was changed into the wine of the Christian; the

type was changed into the antitype; the figure
into the reality; the shadow into the substance.
Then the grace of GOD and the truth of GOD
were revealed and brought to us in all the fulness of this last dispensation.

Let me briefly remind you, brethren, of the
chief points in which Grace and Truth are now
brought to us in all their fulness by the Advent
of the SON of GOD.

1. First of all as to Truth.

The full revelation of Divine Truth which is
now brought to us by JESUS CHRIST may be
briefly summed up in those two great doctrines
which are so well stated in the Athanasian
Creed, viz., those of the Trinity and the Incarnation. These were not revealed to the
Saints of former ages as they are now unto
us.

At the Baptism of the LORD JESUS it was
that the doctrine of the Three Persons began
to be openly revealed upon earth; and by the
command of the LORD Himself we are all now
baptized into the Threefold Name.

Now also the great Mystery of Godliness,
even GOD the SON made Man, has been openly
revealed; "We have seen Him with our eyes,"
writes S. John, "we have looked upon Him;
our very hands have touched Him."

Now therefore, brethren, we know the truth

of the Ever-blessed Trinity; now we know also
the truth of the Incarnation of the Eternal
Word, the Union of the Godhead and the
Manhood in One Person, the adorable Person
of JESUS CHRIST.

And this knowledge changes and transfigures
with heavenly glory all our knowledge.   Here
is contained all the fulness of the Truth of
GOD, even in the Trinity and the Incarnation.

If time permitted, brethren, we might consider our present knowledge of all those great
Articles of Divine Truth which depend upon
these two and follow from them, which were
revealed to the Saints of GOD only in types and
figures,—namely, such as the Atoning Sacrifice of the Lamb of GOD, finished in Blood and
Death on the Cross at Calvary; His Resurrection
in a spiritual body from the dead; His Ascension
in that body to the Throne of His Kingdom;
His ever-abiding Priesthood before the FATHER,
where He is the Lamb as it were slain in sacrifice in the midst of the Throne; and lastly,
the Opening of the Kingdom of Heaven upon
earth at the Coming of the HOLY GHOST.

In all these particulars we have now given us
the fulness of truth, so that even the children of
our school who know the Apostles' Creed have
received the revelation of truth as it is in JESUS

far more abundantly than any of the Saints of old ever did.

2. But let me now remind you, brethren, that not only the fulness of Truth, but also the fulness of Grace has been brought to us by the Advent of the LORD from Heaven.

This fulness of grace, brethren, is given unto us through the Incarnation of the SON of GOD, and through our union or membership with Him as our new Divine Head, the Second Adam; and through His present Priesthood before the FATHER; and through the coming of the HOLY GHOST.

For on His Ascension in our nature into the Presence of the FATHER, our LORD obtained for us *new gifts of grace,* such as had never before been poured out upon the children of men. And on the coming of the HOLY GHOST these new gifts began to be communicated to us; for then the Kingdom of Heaven was opened upon earth to all who believed.

What then, brethren, are these new gifts of grace which are now ministered unto us by the HOLY GHOST?

Time will permit us to consider only those special gifts which are communicated unto us by the HOLY GHOST in the two great Sacraments of CHRIST.

In the first Sacrament of CHRIST we are

made members of the Second Adam; members
of the Mystical Body of CHRIST; members of
that Body of which CHRIST Himself is the
Divine Life-giving Head.

This is a new gift of grace, which, it is plain,
none of the Saints ever possessed before the
LORD was made the Second Adam. It never
was said of any of the Saints before the Advent
of GOD in the flesh: "What, know ye not
that your bodies are the members of CHRIST?"
But now this gift of grace is obtained for us
and brought to us, even that we should be
made members of CHRIST.

Then, brethren, in the other great Sacrament
of the Gospel dispensation, we are fed with the
spiritual food of the most Blessed Body and
Blood of CHRIST, without which, our LORD
expressly reveals to us, we have now "no life
in us."

By this new gift of grace we are made one
with CHRIST, and CHRIST one with us; we are
made to dwell in CHRIST, and CHRIST in us.
It is by means of this communication to us of
His Living and Life-giving Body and Blood
that our union with our Divine Head is now
continually preserved unto the glories of an
immortal resurrection.

To none of the Saints of former ages, it is
plain, was this gift of grace ever given. To

none of them was it ever *once* said, as it is now
so often said to you and me, brethren, " Take,
eat, this is My Body."

Having then, brethren, now received the
last, the fullest revelation of the grace and of
the truth of God, by the Advent of the Son of
God, and by the coming of the Holy Ghost,
O let us ever bear in mind our greater responsibility.

Of us, most certainly, God is expecting the
better, the richer, the higher fruits of grace
and truth. O what is it, brethren, to " walk
worthy of God," Who has now thus called us
to His Kingdom and to His glory? What is
it to "walk worthy of the Lord unto all
pleasing ?"

If God could appeal to His people of old,
and say, " What more could I have done to My
vineyard, that I have not done in it ?" how
much more may He appeal to us ! What more
could God have done for us than He has done ?
What greater gifts of truth and of grace could
God have given us than He has given us ?
What other revelation of truth and of grace
could God have given us more great and
glorious than that which He has given us by
His Son and by His Spirit?

How then, brethren, are you profiting by
that truth and by that grace which have been

so freely revealed to us by the Advent of GOD our SAVIOUR, and communicated to us by the coming of the HOLY GHOST? O what a good thing would it be for too many of us, brethren, if we had been born before the Advent of GOD in the flesh, before these new gifts of truth and of grace had been poured forth! O what a good thing for many of us if we had been born in some heathen nation!

By what fruits of righteousness and goodness and truth are you glorifying GOD? Are you, brethren, growing in grace and in the knowledge of the LORD? Are you growing up into Him in all things, Who is our New Divine Head, so that in the overwhelming glory of His Second Advent you may not be confounded, but may be able to rejoice with exceeding great joy for ever?

SERMON XI.

CHRISTMAS FESTIVITIES.

𝔉ourth 𝔖unday in 𝔄dvent.

ISAIAH v. 12.

"AND THE HARP, AND THE VIOL, THE TABRET, AND PIPE,
AND WINE, ARE IN THEIR FEASTS; BUT THEY REGARD NOT
THE WORK OF THE LORD, NEITHER CONSIDER THE OPERA-
TION OF HIS HANDS."

As it was in the days of the holy prophets, brethren, so it is still. The world robs the Church of her sacred seasons. Men are so much taken up with worldly business or pleasure, that the work of the LORD is not regarded, the operation of His hands is not considered.

It is specially so, as we all know, to a very great extent indeed, at Christmas time. Even with the more serious amongst us it is so, to a very considerable extent.

At this holy Season the world, the flesh, and

the devil all fight against us with more than usual strength. The world robs the Church of her most sacred seasons, the customs of the world distract our attention from the very greatest works of God.

With too many this holy Season of Christmas is altogether diverted from its proper purpose. So very much so, that in many cases to wish any one "a merry Christmas" only means to wish him an abundance of merely worldly merriment. And indeed, in many cases, it means worse than this a great deal; it means abundance of sinful indulgences: so very much so, that it is to be feared that Christmas time is the time most full of sin of all the year.

The occasion of the coming of the Son of God into the world for the very purpose of saving us from our sins, is made the very occasion for indulging in more sin than usual.

How sad and shameful this is, brethren. How displeasing before God that we should indulge in mere natural mirth, in mere sensual enjoyment, at the very season which is set apart for celebrating the glory of God's greatest work; for rejoicing in the mightiest and most amazing operation of His hands.

Permit me, therefore, brethren, to warn you against this common evil—the evil of indulging merely in worldly feasting and entertainment at the holy Season of Christmas.

There is no evil in making a great feast on suitable occasions. We all know that our LORD Himself honoured with His presence and with His first miracle, a feast made on the occasion of a marriage.

There is no evil in natural affection. If we be without natural affection, we are below the very beasts that perish. Yet we know who has said, "If any man love father or mother more than Me, he is not worthy of Me." There is no evil in attending to our farm and merchandize. But was it not evil when those people in the parable went to their farm and their merchandize at the very time when the king invited them to the marriage feast?

There is no evil in rejoicing with natural joy when families meet together in mutual affection and love. But was it not evil that Martha should busy herself about mere household duties when the LORD Himself had arrived at her house? Was it not evil that she should put her household duties before the presence of the LORD?

Even so, brethren, is it not evil, to be all taken up in family cares, or in family affections, or in worldly feasting, or in mere natural pleasures, at the very time when we are called upon to celebrate the glory of the greatest

H

work of God, to consider the mightiest operation of His hands?

O let not any of us be guilty of this sinful disregard of God, this sinful abuse of a holy season, this Christmas time. Oh let not the world rob any of us of the special blessing of this sacred season. Oh let not the angels of Heaven sorrowfully say of any of us, "The harp, and the viol, the tabret, and pipe, and wine, are in their feasts; but they regard not the work of the Lord, neither do they consider the operation of His hands."

Let us all rather consider, brethren, the two special duties, the two spiritual privileges, the two heavenly blessings, which this happy week brings to us.

You all know, brethren, what they are, but it is fit that I should remind you of them.

One is, that on Christmas Day you should all come to Church, in order to celebrate publicly, before God, with special worship, praise, and thanksgiving, His great work, His amazing work, the mighty operation of His hands, His infinite grace towards us, the revelation of His eternal Love, in sending forth into this world from His glory His only Begotten and Eternal Son, in giving us this His most unspeakable Gift.

It is written, "When He bringeth in the

First-begotten into the world, He saith, And
let all the Angels of GOD worship Him."

Much more reason have we to worship Him,
brethren, in all the lowliness of His human
Nativity. GOD said, you see, "Let all the
angels," not one was wanting, we may be sure,
on such an occasion.

And should one of us be wanting? Surely
he that fails to worship the LORD of Glory,
lying on His manger-throne, is not fit to be
called a Christian. He that does not consider,
does not regard this work of GOD, surely cannot be easily excused.

No one then who calls himself a Christian
should fail on any account, except real necessity, to keep holy Christmas Day, to honour
the human birthday of the Redeemer of
the world. No one surely can be worthy even
of the name of a Christian who refuses or
neglects to celebrate with holy worship before
GOD the Birth of His Eternal SON into our
human family; the very foundation of all our
hope, the only real and true cause of happiness
and joy which we sinners have.

Oh let none of us turn the special grace and
blessing of Christmas time, as many do, into a
special sin and curse. But let us all prepare
ourselves the best we can for our visit to the
LORD from Heaven, on the day of His birth

into our family, to worship Him lying on His most lowly throne, even in the manger, in the stable at Bethlehem.

The other duty, privilege, and blessing, brethren, which this happy week brings to you, of which it is my duty to remind you, is the reception of the Holy Communion of the Body and Blood of CHRIST. For this indeed is our true Christmas Feast. Christmas without this cannot be Christmas.

For what would you say, brethren, if I were to ask you to meet together at a Harvest Thanksgiving Service in order to praise GOD for giving you corn to make bread with, if you never meant to eat any bread? Or what would you say if some one told you it was enough for the support of your life to believe in the corn; to believe that bread had power to sustain your life and your strength, but that you need not actually receive or eat it?

Even so, brethren, it is not enough that you only hear of the LORD JESUS, that you only believe in Him, but you must also do what He bids you; if you would have life from Him, you must make use of those means of Grace which He has appointed.

Else you will be just like a sick and dying man who says he believes the physician has power to heal his disease and to save him from

death, and yet neglects to take the very medi-
cine which he orders.

For our SAVIOUR came into the world and
was made Man, not only to die for us, but as
well, to give Himself to us, to be our indwelling Life.

And in this Holy Communion He thus communicates Himself to us, to be in us. And on
Christmas Day, oh consider with what lowliness and gentleness He comes to us, and presents Himself to us, if we will receive Him.

Let me then invite you, in the name of
your SAVIOUR, brethren, to attend to this duty,
to avail yourselves of this privilege, to receive
this heavenly blessing on Christmas Day. If
you refuse the invitation of GOD to the heavenly
banquet which He offers you on Christmas
Day, then I entreat of you one favour, for the
good of your own soul,—not to indulge in any
feast at home. Do not turn your back on the
LORD's Table and then go to your own table.
Do not feast your poor dying body and starve
your immortal soul. Do not be so extremely
foolish in the sight of all heaven.

Or if you will not grant me this favour, then
I beg of you that when you sit down at the
feast at your own table, in neglect of the feast
that GOD offers, you will call to mind the words
of my text.

But come to Church, I beseech you, brethren, on Christmas Day, to keep your SAVIOUR's human Birthday, to celebrate the Nativity of the LORD from Heaven, to honour the Advent of the SON of GOD, to worship your LORD lying on His most lowly throne.

And also come to receive Him in the most Holy Communion of His Body and Blood. Come to receive That which is Meat indeed and That which is Drink indeed from off the Table of the LORD, for the spiritual food and sustenance of the very life of your soul in CHRIST. Come to be made partakers of the very benefit of the Incarnation and Advent of the SON of GOD.

SERMON XII.

THE SIGN OF THE PRESENCE.

Fourth Sunday in Advent.

S. LUKE II. 12.

"THIS SHALL BE A SIGN UNTO YOU."

WHAT is filling up your mind, brethren, at this holy season of the Christian year? What is filling your soul with more amazement than ever? Is it the great mystery of godliness, "GOD manifest in the flesh?"

This, brethren, is the mystery of all mysteries; this is the miracle of all miracles; this is the new work that GOD has wrought for you and for me. This is the amazing foundation of our Christian religion, the Incarnation of the Second Person of the eternal Godhead, the Nativity of the LORD from Heaven in our human family, the Birth of the Eternal SON of GOD of the Blessed Virgin Mary.

Who of us can ever entertain any thoughts worthy of this glorious mystery? Who of us has ever yet given any due honour to the human Birthday of our great Redeemer?

Let me endeavour to serve you, this evening, (through the mercy and grace of God) by helping you to prepare yourselves for your Christmas visit to the eternal Son of God as He lies on His manger-throne in the cattle-stall, born of the Blessed Virgin Mary.

For the design of the Church in appointing the various holy seasons of the Christian year is this, to help us to live over again all the chief events concerning our Lord, so that we may learn to believe in Him, and to follow Him, and to love Him, ever more and more.

Let us then now go back in spirit to the time just before the Lord's Advent. The fulness of the time was now come, and God would send forth His eternal Son into the world. The promised Redeemer of the world was just about to appear. The Lord from Heaven was just about to be manifested here upon earth.

Now, let me ask you, brethren, What sign should you have expected, when the Son of God should thus come down from Heaven? What sign should you have expected would be given, by which you might be able to know Him when you should see Him?

What loud call, what great and wonderful sign (do you think) would GOD give from Heaven to call the attention of the whole world to guide them to the place, that all might know and be certain that "This is the SON of GOD: Here is the Presence of the LORD from Heaven: This is He."

Call to mind, brethren, how this was in old time. When GOD would reveal His Presence, in any special manner, here upon earth, in former times, what open signs of it were given?

At mount Sinai, for instance, when the LORD came down, the signs of His Presence were so very overpowering and terrible, that even Moses said, "I exceedingly fear and quake."

When Isaiah beheld, in a vision, the glory of the LORD's Presence, he was so overcome with fear and reverence, that he exclaimed, "Woe is me, I am undone; for mine eyes have seen the King, the LORD of Hosts."

And if you will call to mind the history of the passage through the Red Sea, and of the passage through Jordan, you will understand what the Psalmist means when he says, "What aileth thee, O thou sea, that thou fleddest, and thou Jordan, that thou wast driven back? Ye mountains, that ye skipped like rams, and ye little hills like young sheep? Tremble, thou earth at the presence of the LORD, at the presence of the GOD of Israel."

What sign, then, brethren, of overpowering grandeur, what sign of majesty divine, should you have expected would have been given from Heaven, by which all the world might know at once the Advent of the SON of GOD, the actual Presence of the LORD from Heaven, the sending forth of GOD's eternal SON?

What sign should you have naturally expected by which all the world might perceive and know at once "This is the LORD from Heaven's highest throne: This is GOD our SAVIOUR?"

Might we not have expected that the Advent of the LORD from Heaven would have been attended by some great open sign of His Divine power and glory; that perhaps twelve legions of the mightiest Archangels of Heaven should have been around Him in all their splendour of glory; or that, at the very least, all the princes and nobles of the earth would have attended Him, to minister unto Him of all the best that earth could afford?

But, brethren, you know how often those words of S. Paul are fulfilled: "GOD chooses the foolish things of the world to confound the wise, and the weak things of the world to confound the things that are mighty."

The prophet Isaiah prophesied concerning this sign, saying, "Ask thee a sign of the LORD thy GOD; ask it either in the depth below or in the height above."

But who could venture to ask it? Who but GOD Himself could give the sign of the Advent of the LORD? GOD Himself, therefore, now again speaks from Heaven by His Angel, and says, "This shall be a sign unto you."

This is the sign by which those shepherds were to seek, and to find, and to know the actual Presence of the LORD from Heaven, the SAVIOUR of the world. Such a sign, brethren, as humble faith alone could receive, entirely destitute of all that the world counts grand. "This shall be a sign unto you," a sign by means of which you shall go and find Him, and know that it is He.

"Ye shall find the Babe wrapped in swaddling clothes, lying in a manger."

O what a strange, unexpected sign, exceeding in lowliness as much as we thought it would have exceeded in grandeur; even a manger; by which to find the Birthplace of the LORD from Heaven; even a Little Infant; by which to know the actual Presence of GOD.

No heavenly glory around Him too dazzling for human eye. Not even one Angel to be seen by His side. No thunderings, no

lightnings, no rolling earthquake, no sharp
fiery sword of justice by His side.

The sign of the Presence of GOD our SA-
VIOUR is nothing but a Little Child lying in a
manger borrowed from the cattle.

If you were to judge, brethren, only by
natural reason, only by your bodily senses,
you might well say, "Can this be He? Can
this be the Birthplace of the LORD from
Heaven? Can this be the Advent of GOD in
the flesh? Is this the sending forth of GOD's
Eternal SON? Only a Little Child! and that
Child lying in a manger!"

But, brethren, guided by faith in the words
spoken by the Angel of GOD, and by faith in
the words spoken by the prophets of GOD, we
shall go and see and know and believe and be
sure that underneath this Sign of weakness,
and poverty, and silence, and exceeding great
humility, beneath the Form of this Little
Child, there is "verily and indeed" the actual
Presence, the real Presence of the LORD from
Heaven.

And now in the meanwhile we may well
consider one or two lessons which we may learn
from this Sign.

First of all let us learn, brethren, that we
can never find the knowledge of the mysteries
of GOD by the strength of human reason.

Unless we seek by faith, faith depending upon the Word of God, we shall never find the knowledge of wisdom.

If we judge by sight or sense, we shall never discern the Presence of the Lord. We must follow the humble shepherds, who believed the Word of God spoken by the Angel, and being guided by the Sign which the Angel gave them, found the Presence of the Lord our Saviour.

They did not stumble at the lowliness of the outward Sign. Their faith prevailed against their sight. And so in that Little Child they were able to discern the Presence of God.

Now here, brethren, if you will only consider it, here indeed was the greatest of all great Sacraments. Here the visible and the invisible were united together. Here heaven and earth were joined together. Here God and Man were united in one Person. Here the lowest was joined to the highest; for here, beneath a very humble earthly visible Sign, there was the real and true Presence of God Incarnate.

Thus it is, let us then learn, brethren, in that great Sacrament of the Gospel, which our Lord has now ordained for our constant use.

There is a humble, lowly, earthly sign for

the outward and visible part of the Sacrament —only bread and wine; very poor and lowly in the eyes of the world, so that the world in general passes by, in the blindness and in the rudeness of unbelief.

But what is the inward invisible part of the Sacrament, seen only by the eye of faith?

Beneath that humble outward sign, we know, and believe, and are sure (by faith in the words of the LORD Himself) that here is the actual Presence of the Body and Blood of GOD Incarnate; for His words are, "This is My Body," "This is My Blood."

The world said *then* concerning that Little Child lying in that manger, "Can this be GOD? O no, it is only the Son of the Carpenter."

So the world says *now* of this Sacrament. "Can this be the Body of GOD Incarnate? O no, it is only a little piece of bread."

But let this Sign of the LORD's Presence, brethren, teach us another lesson. It is this, that our LORD comes not to terrify us, but to comfort us; not to destroy us, but to save us; not to drive us away, but to draw us very near to Him; He comes in all the meekness, and gentleness, and tenderness He could, so that not the most wretched sinner amongst us need be frightened from Him.

The Sign shows us at once that GOD our

SAVIOUR comes to receive the poor in spirit, to bless the humble and the meek, to comfort them that mourn, to bless every sinner who will come unto Him.

But now, lastly, let me again beseech you to remember to keep the LORD's human Birthday with all the reverence and devotion in your power. Too often the world completely robs the Church of her Holy Seasons, turning them all into occasions of mere carnal mirth or worldly pleasure. Just as the prophet said it would be, "The harp, and the viol, the tabret and pipe, and wine are in their feasts, but they regard not the work of the LORD, neither consider the operation of His hands."

O let it not be thus, brethren, with any of you. Show your faith in GOD your SAVIOUR by keeping His human birthday. Show your faith in your SAVIOUR by worshipping Him, even in the midst of all His weakness and littleness, and poverty, and silence, even as a Little Child lying in a manger.

Let it be some little sign of your love towards your SAVIOUR that you keep sacred His human Birthday, when He was laid so low, in order that you might be drawn very near to Him in all gentleness and tenderness. O come, brethren, to the LORD JESUS on His own human Birthday; a day that He so well

remembers; a day on which He gives you
leave to draw near unto Him as He lies upon
His manger-throne in the cattle stall. Come
and worship the Holy Child JESUS on His
Birthday. Come and lay down your heart
at His feet, and beseech Him to take it and to
cleanse it, and to keep it His for ever.

And above all, let it be some little sign of
your faith and of your love towards Him, that
you worship GOD on His human birthday in
that Chief Act of worship which the LORD
Himself commands, in which He grants His
Presence under so lowly and humble an outward Sign; in which He comes to give Himself to us, in all the gentleness and meekness of His first Advent, that we may be made
partakers of all the benefits of His Incarnation.

Now unto Him, once for us lying in the
manger, now reigning on the Throne of the
FATHER, be all humblest thanks, all highest
praise.

SERMON XIII.

THE LORD'S HUMAN BIRTHDAY.

Christmas Day.

S. LUKE II. 15.

"LET US NOW GO EVEN TO BETHLEHEM."

EVERY word here, brethren, is now to us most full of meaning. "Let *us* go." Let others go where they please; let others keep their own poor birthdays. Let us keep the birthday of the LORD JESUS. Let us go to Bethlehem.

"Let us *now* go." Even this very hour; without any delay; even as those shepherds did, "with haste." For who that seeks the Presence of the LORD with slothfulness will ever be able to find Him? Who that has other things to do first will ever find GOD?

"Let us now *go*;" because sitting still at

I

home has never yet brought any one to see
the glory of GOD in the face of JESUS CHRIST.
No one has ever yet apprehended the great
mystery of godliness without going "even to
Bethlehem."

This word "*even*" implies some difficulty.
It is an easy thing for you, brethren, to sit
still and listen to the wondrous story of the
LORD's Nativity, and then to forget it all, just
as you would some cunningly devised fable.
But to go there, as we ought, to see Him there
by faith, and there to worship Him, and there
to receive Him as our very LORD and SAVIOUR,
all this is not easy.

But, brethren, to believe in *Bethlehem's*
wondrous story, to the saving of your soul, this,
remember, is the one thing of your life.   If you
fail in this, all is lost.

Let us then now arise and go in heart and
mind even to Bethlehem, with all the little faith
we have, and with all the humility we can ex-
ercise.   Let us go and pay a visit of faith and
of love to GOD our SAVIOUR on this His human birthday.

Come then, brethren, all poor and trembling
sinners.   Come, all meek and humble-minded
poor.   Come, all ye who labour and are heavy
laden.   Come, all ye who cry and pray unto
GOD with a broken and a contrite spirit.   You

need not be frightened, brethren; the Angel from Heaven says, " Fear not!"

For you are not going to see the dread tribunal of your Judge. You are not going to see the splendour of the majesty of His eternal Godhead. I am not asking you to ascend up into Heaven to see Him as He is there, but only to come to the little country town of Bethlehem to see Him as He is there.

The Angel of GOD has given us the sign by means of which we shall know Him when we see Him,—a sign so humble and lowly, that there is nothing in it to terrify the very weakest one amongst us. The Angel tells us, that we must search for a little Infant, and that Infant lying in a manger; and in that little Child, lying on that lowly throne, we shall see GOD manifest in the flesh.

The town of Bethlehem is quiet, for it is night, the busy day of the taxing is over. The inns are all full of strangers. No one thinks of the two weary strangers who came from Nazareth; they looked like plain country people, wayworn and poor. There was no room, of course, in the inn, for such kind of travellers. The good man of the inn would say of course such words as these: "O, my house is full; there is no room here for such poor people as you." And then perhaps he looked at them

again, and then he might say : "Well, the
poor young woman looks ill, you may take
shelter in that cattle-shed, if you like."

So it came to pass, brethren, that the Lord
was born in a stable, and laid in a manger.
The holy Joseph and the Blessed Virgin would
not murmur for their own sakes ; but did it
not pity them to lay the Holy Infant in such a
poor and lowly bed ?

This is a plain and true picture, brethren, of
the usual manner in which the world treats
God. Anything is good enough for God. Are
you, brethren, treating God any better ?

But now, brethren, come and let us enter
into the cave, or cattle-shed. O come, let us
worship and fall down, and kneel before the
Lord our Maker. O come in, and behold the
Holy Child Jesus, and say with all the little
faith you have, " My Lord and my God."

Behold the Nativity of the Lord from Heaven. Look down into the manger, and behold
the Divine Infant.

Behold those little Hands, so weak and so
little, now lifted up towards His human Mother's loving face ; yet at the same moment
upholding all the worlds of the universe.

Listen to that gentle Voice, the voice of
human infancy, breaking the silence of mid-
night, moving all the depths of the Blessed

Virgin's heart; that same Voice which will one day soon, brethren, say to you and me, "Come, ye blessed," or "Depart, ye cursed."

Behold those little Feet, soon going to carry Him through the cities and villages of Judæa to call sinners to repentance, soon going to be pierced and broken with the iron spike, soon going to ascend the highest throne of Heaven.

Behold the adorable Countenance, in which you may see the reflection of the Love of God, which fills the Blessed Mother's heart with an unceasing ecstasy of delight; at the sight of which, beaten and livid with blows, defiled with blood and spitting, pale in death, the Blessed Virgin will soon be pierced through and through with the sharpest sword of affliction; at the open vision of which, radiant in the glory of the Father, all the blessed company of Heaven are now filled with full torrents of delight; at the first moment's sight of which, brethren, you and I shall know our doom.

Here, then, brethren, even at Bethlehem, is the Miracle of all miracles; here is the profound Mystery of the Divine Incarnation openly revealed before you. Here is, to sight and sense, only a little child; here is, to faith, the Eternal Son of God. Here is the greatest of all great Sacraments,—for here is verily and indeed the Divine Presence, but hidden under the most lowly sign.

As GOD, His eternal throne is in Heaven; as Man, He is lying in this manger here. As GOD, He is arrayed in glory infinite; here as Man, He is wrapped in those poor mean garments. As GOD, the Heaven of Heavens cannot contain Him; here, as Man, He is contained in this narrow bed.

O eternal amazement of men and Angels! O inconceivable humiliation of the SON of GOD, to be made thus the Son of Mary! Here Heaven and earth are joined together; here GOD and Man are united in One Person.

Come then, brethren, all of you, draw near to Him Who thus draws near to you in such exceeding great humility. This is the human birthday of the LORD and SAVIOUR. Well He remembers Bethlehem to-day.

To-day, we may be very sure, " He receiveth sinners," without one word of chiding, without one look of rebuke, as He lies upon His manger-throne in the cattle-stall. O come then, every one of you, brethren, come and lay down your heart at His feet, and beseech Him to take it, and to cleanse it, and to renew it, and to sanctify it, to make it His own for ever, so that you may be eternally blessed in Him.

O yield your heart to GOD your SAVIOUR,

trust in His love, believe in His love, give Him your heart, and as He is GOD, He will fill it with large measure of His own brightness, and purity, and peace, and love, and joy, and glory for ever.

But one other truth requires our attention this morning, brethren. There remains yet, that (in a most true and real sense) we should this very morning "now go even to Bethlehem."

Names are never given to persons or to places at random in Holy Scripture. Bethlehem is a Hebrew word, and it is in English, "the House of Bread." Not without Divine foreknowledge was JESUS born at Bethlehem. For He Who came down from Heaven said, "I am the Bread of Life." He came not only to suffer and die for us, but just as much to give Himself to us, and be in us, the very food and sustenance of Life in us, even the very Bread of Life.

And for this purpose He has ordained a great Sacrament for us, as the channel through which He gives us this very grace. Here is our true Bethlehem, even at the Table of the LORD. Here is that breaking of Bread which the LORD commands. Here He Himself spreads a Table for us, even here in the wilderness of this world, where He Himself offers us that which He says is Meat indeed, and that which He says is drink indeed. Here the outward and visible sign is humble and lowly, even Bread, but beneath this sign is hidden the Presence of the Body of our LORD. For the LORD Himself speaks and says, "This is My Body." And S. Paul says, "The Bread which we break, is the Communion of the Body of CHRIST."

Here then, brethren, the LORD Himself offers Himself to us as the very Bread of Life. This is the true Manna which came down from Heaven itself. This is the Living and the Life-giving Bread. Here is our true Bethlehem.

O let us then even now go to Bethlehem, however poor, and weak, and unworthy we are; for the LORD to-day most surely graciously receiveth sinners without any word of rebuke. Here He gives nothing less than Himself to every penitent believing soul, under the most humble and lowly signs.

Let us therefore draw near with faith,—faith resting on the word of the LORD: "Take, eat, this is My Body; drink ye all of This, for This is My Blood." And again: "Whoso eateth My Flesh and drinketh My Blood, dwelleth in Me, and I in him."

SERMON XIV.

THE HOLY NATIVITY.

Christmas Day.

S. MATTH. I. 18.

"NOW THE BIRTH OF JESUS CHRIST WAS ON THIS WISE."

THERE have been many wonderful things in this world of ours, brethren, but not one of them ever half so wonderful as "the Birth of JESUS CHRIST." There have been many great events in the world, which we commemorate year by year, but not one of them has any greatness in comparison of that which we commemorate to-day, "the birth of JESUS CHRIST."

You may read in books of fiction many surprising stories, but you can never read anything half so surprising as that which we celebrate to-day, "the Birth of JESUS CHRIST."

For this is the human Birthday of GOD our

Saviour. This is the great and holy day on which the eternal Son of God was born into our human family, and made the Son of the Blessed Virgin Mary.

Every year, brethren, you have heard this history. Every Christmas Day we have celebrated the Birthday of the Lord from Heaven. But when have we ever thought of it as we ought? The more we think of it the more wonderful it ever seems. The oftener we hear of it, the more wonderful, the more new, it ever seems.

Though you have often heard the story of the Lord's Nativity, brethren, yet I am sure you will wish to hear it again this evening. There is nothing new in it. It is the same story, year by year, and it will be the same now for ever. But who ever grows tired of the story of the Birth of Jesus Christ?

As well might any one grow tired of the light of the sun, or of the deep blue sky, or of the grandeur of the ocean, or of the calm moonlight, or of the very joys of Heaven, as of the story of " the Birth of Jesus Christ."

Of course, if you had never heard of it before, you would not be able to believe it. You would take up your books and throw them at my head, or you would take up your hats and walk out of Church, at hearing me tell you such a cunningly devised fable.

Will you try and listen to it, as if you had never heard it before?

GOD orders all things, both in Heaven and in earth, in perfect wisdom, from the beginning to the ending, by His mighty Providence ruling over all.

Now the fulness of the time was come for the birth of the promised Redeemer of the world. So in unconscious obedience to the will of GOD, Cæsar Augustus, the Emperor of Rome, issued a decree that all the world should be taxed.

Now Joseph and Mary lived at Nazareth. But in obedience to the Emperor's decree, they went to Bethlehem, the city of David, because they were of the family of David. And so the prophecy was fulfilled, which said that the CHRIST should be born at Bethlehem.

After some days' journey then, for it was eighty miles or more, Mary and Joseph arrived at Bethlehem, at nightfall, way-worn and tired.

The Blessed Virgin (we may be sure) was little fit for that journey from Nazareth to Bethlehem. Other women, of course, would have made an excuse, and stayed at home, just as so many women in this village always make excuses, and say that they have so many household duties to attend to, that they cannot come to Church.

How many careless men, too, always make excuses and stay at home, instead of obeying the call of duty, instead of not minding trouble when it is the time of GOD's holy worship.

When the bell rings for the worship of GOD, O how many people stay at home, despising the Church of GOD, dishonouring the Altar of GOD, breaking Christian unity, hurting their own souls, making a heap of silly, vain excuses. Little blessing are such careless triflers with GOD likely to find. For it is written, "GOD is a rewarder of them that diligently seek Him."

Think then, brethren, of Mary and Joseph thus in the streets of Bethlehem at nightfall seeking for a lodging. The cold, early evening of winter was closing in. Mary and Joseph seek in vain to find a lodging. For the Emperor's decree had brought many strangers there; the little town was quite full.

Mary and Joseph perhaps were a little late. The Blessed Virgin had not been able to travel so far very fast. All the lodgings were taken.

S. Joseph was one of the greatest saints, made fit to be the foster-father of the LORD. Mary was above all, the first of saints, made fit to be the Mother of Him Who is GOD.

She was bearing within her the Incarnate GOD Himself, the eternal WORD, the Maker and Sovereign of all in that town of Bethlehem, the Judge of all mankind.

But when they came to Bethlehem that night there was no room for them. The little town was full. The town people were all taken up about this decree, and they were all in a state of excitement at the great number of strangers that had arrived.

The officers of Cæsar Augustus were very busy making the census, enrolling all the people for the taxing. Those officers of state were the great people there. And they and the rich visitors had, of course, engaged all the best that the inn could give. The private houses would be full of relations from the country. Every one was busy, and every room was engaged.

So these two plain country people from Nazareth, that humble carpenter from Galilee, that youthful, lowly Mother, that hidden WORD, there was no room found for them.

We can easily fancy the landlord of the inn looking at their humble, way-worn appearance, and then speaking some such words as these, "O, my inn is quite full, every room is engaged. I cannot take you in. There's no room here for such as you."

But then, perhaps, he looked at the Blessed Virgin, and he would see that she looked ill, and so he told them that they might take shelter in the cattle-yard if they liked.

At the beginning and at the ending of His life in this world, brethren, it was just the same. Just as no one in Jerusalem took Him in during that last week, or gave Him food, so that He had each night to go out of the city and find a lodging at Bethany, so at His Birth He could hardly find a place where to be born. He was thrust out among the cattle of the stall.

And, brethren, do you not see plainly enough how it is still? The spirit of Bethlehem is still the spirit of the world, a world that has forgotten GOD. " He was in the world, and the world was made by Him, and the world knew Him not."

O, brethren, consider, how are we for ever shutting our doors against GOD. GOD comes to us repeatedly, but we do not know Him. GOD often knocks at our door, but we do not know it. GOD lives close to us in His House, but we do not know it. Our SAVIOUR is standing knocking at our door, and we pay no attention, so He goes away. We only find it out when He is gone. O what a grievous loss it is to us to be so blind and rude.

So we go on, brethren, most of us, most of
our lifetime, meeting GOD every day, and not
knowing Him. Has it not been so in this
parish with many this morning? When I did
all I could to distinguish the one only service
ordained by CHRIST Himself, most of the people
of this parish knew it not. Most turned their
backs upon it, not knowing that to turn from
the Sacrament of CHRIST is to turn from
CHRIST Himself.

Well, Joseph and Mary (I suppose) were
not much surprised. They whose minds are
stayed by faith on GOD are not much troubled
about these outward things. Joseph, perhaps,
calmly looked on Mary, and they quietly and
uncomplainingly, and even thankfully, went to
the cattle-shed.

As it is well said, "This world affords no
home for the saints of GOD." This world
shuts the door against GOD. Bethlehem was
full of gaiety that night, full of glittering
lights, and of merry songs, and of loud music;
full of feasting and dancing.

A poor couple (as the world would think)
came in on foot that night from Nazareth, unknown and unprovided. They had no friends
to receive them, they sought shelter and rest
with the ox and the ass of the stable. Anything was good enough for GOD! The refuse

of what we leave, the crumbs from our table, this is what man generally gives to God.

So then, brethren, it came to pass that Jesus Christ was born in a stable, and laid in a manger.

Now then, brethren, may we (do you think) may we look in? May we look in and see Him lying on His humble throne? Have you faith enough to support you?

Behold with sad amazement, brethren, behold the poor nursery of the King of kings. There are the beasts, here is the manger. Look at the straw and hay.

But now see, in the midst of all, Mary looks upon the Face of the Divine Infant. Long had she been ardently desiring to see the face of the Holy Child, and now she beholds it. Again and again she looks. The sunlight of that Countenance doubtless filled the Blessed Mother with the most unspeakable ecstasy of delight.

The Holy Child opens His human eyes, and looks round. He beholds the cave, and the cattle, and the manger; the grand place that the world gave Him to be born in. He beholds His human Mother with unutterable love, and the holy Joseph with deepest affection.

Then also that part of the great mystery of godliness is fulfilled, God manifest in the flesh is "seen of Angels," seen by the Angels in a condition lower than themselves. For as S. Paul writes, "When GOD brought in the First-Begotten into the world, He said, Let all the Angels of GOD worship Him." Then, therefore, all the thrones, and dominions, and powers, and ranks, and orders of the Heavenly Host were bowed down, in profoundest amazement and reverence before the Divine Infant.

But on earth beneath all was calm and quiet. No thunder pealed, no lightning flashed, no earthquake stirred. For it was all foreordained in the eternal will of GOD. All this was foreseen from all eternity.

And when the fulness of the time was come, GOD thus fulfilled His great promise. GOD thus sent forth His eternal SON into this world, born at Bethlehem of the Blessed Virgin Mary.

To-day, therefore, throughout the world, the Church celebrates the Birthday of the LORD JESUS. To-day all the faithful worship GOD by the side of the manger throne of the Divine Infant. And to-day therefore, brethren, surely all the hosts of Heaven celebrate afresh the glory of this mystery.

To-day, brethren, the LORD JESUS Himself, although now seated in glory, at the right hand of the FATHER, is remembering His human

Birthday. To-day He remembers the cattle stall, He remembers the manger. To-day He is very ready to be gracious to all humble, penitent sinners. To-day we may say with great certainty, "He receiveth sinners."

O let us then, this very night, take advantage of His great humility, and cast ourselves down in the dust, by the lowly throne of GOD our SAVIOUR, laying down our hearts at His feet.

For here is One, born into our human family, who is able, who is willing, who is longing to relieve us of all our miseries, to fill us with the fulness of joy, and to lift us up into His own eternal glory.

Here is joy for every age and for every nation. Here is glad tidings of great joy for every poor sinful child of Adam who is cast down, bent down, broken down, undone by sin. O let none of us despise our own mercies. He calls us to-day, without voice, to come very near to Him, to approach Him on His lowly throne, to trust ourselves to His love, and to yield our hearts to Him, to be His for ever.

Will you then go home now, brethren, and ponder in your hearts this wondrous story of the birth of JESUS CHRIST? And this very night fall down on your knees by the side of the manger, in the cattle stall of Bethlehem.

And I beseech you do not be dumb to the LORD
JESUS. O say something to Him; crowd in
among the throng around His manger throne
this night; ask for some blessing from your
humble GOD.

SERMON XV.

THE MYSTERY OF BETHLEHEM.

Christmas Day.

S. Luke ii. 16.

"And they came with haste; and found Mary and
Joseph; and the Babe lying in a manger."

THE Mystery which God permits us to celebrate to-day, brethren, is indeed most infinitely
great. It is far beyond all our narrow thoughts,
it is far above all our feeble powers. We have
heard of it all our life long; we have been fa-
miliar with it from our childhood. But who of
us has ever believed it, ever thought of it, ever
rejoiced in it, as he ought? Who of us has
ever yet kept the Lord's birthday as he
ought?

Let me beseech you all, brethren, now to
accompany me, in spirit, to the side of the

lowly throne of GOD our SAVIOUR. Let us go, as the believing shepherds did, " with haste," with eager hearts, with great wonder, with great reverence, with all the little faith we have; above all things, in great humility, to see this thing which is come to pass.

For to-day all believers assemble together at Bethlehem; to-day the Holy Church throughout the world is celebrating the most joyful Nativity of GOD our SAVIOUR.

Let us go too, brethren, with all the company of the faithful, to pay a visit of faith and of love to the LORD our SAVIOUR on this His human birthday. For most surely He expects this from us all to-day.

Who of us would be missing? Who will refuse or neglect to give glory and worship to the LORD on this His human birthday? Is it not well remembered in Heaven above? Does He, the LORD Himself, forget His own lowly throne on that the day of His Nativity? Shall any of us forget it? The more He humbles Himself, so much the more ought we to honour and worship Him.

O come then, brethren, let us worship and fall down, and kneel in the dust before the lowly throne of the LORD our Maker.

First of all, brethren, will you use your *natural senses* only? consider only what you

see before you in the stable at Bethlehem.
What do you see with the eye of sense?

Here is S. Joseph, the carpenter; here is the
Virgin Mary, whom all generations, by the command of the HOLY GHOST, do now call Blessed;
here too, you may see, if you look round, the
ox and the ass, fit emblems of labour and
patience; and here is a manger, borrowed from
the cattle; and in this poor and lowly cradle
you see a little Child, in all the weakness and
speechlessness and humility of human infancy.

These outward and visible things, brethren,
do not seem very great, nothing very grand,
nothing in them to frighten you, nothing to
drive you away, no, nothing to terrify even a
little child. O no, you will easily say, we are not
afraid of the quiet cattle, we are not afraid of the
humble carpenter, we are not afraid of the lowly
maiden, we are not afraid of that little Child.

The outward and visible part of the Mystery,
brethren, seems humble and lowly indeed,—all
earthly and human. You can see nothing but
only a little Child, wrapped in some poor
clothes, laid on the lowest humblest bed that
could be found, attended by a carpenter and a
holy Jewish maiden, and by some shepherds
from the field, the ox and the ass standing by.
So that if you judge by sight and by sense
only, only according to nature, you might easily

pass it by, as those people at the inn did; you
might easily suppose that there is nothing more
than some poor little child, whom some very
poor people, who had come on foot from Nazareth, had been obliged to lay in a manger for a
bed. And your only remark might be, "Well,
I never saw an infant laid in such a cradle as
that before."

But now, brethren, let us attend, I beseech
you, to the other part of the great Mystery.
Because a Mystery of GOD has two parts,—one
of this earth, but the other of Heaven. One
part to be discerned by the bodily eye, the
other only by faith in the Word of GOD.

Now then, brethren, will you use your *faith?*
Now use all the faith that you possess. Now
let your faith teach you, and enable you to discern the heavenly part of the great Mystery of
Godliness. Now let your faith guide you; let
your faith be stronger than sight, faith enlight-
ened by the Word of GOD, resting on the mes-
sage of the Angel of GOD: "Unto you is born
this day, in the City of David, a SAVIOUR,
which is the CHRIST, the LORD. And this shall
be the sign unto you,"—this is the visible
sign, by means of which you shall know Him
when you see Him,—" ye shall find the Babe
lying in a manger."

Look down, then, brethren, look down again

into that manger, and let your faith be stronger than your sight. For here before you is that very Sign of the Presence of the LORD, which the Angel told you of.

Your sight tells you, here is the manger; your sight tells you, and you need not contradict your sight, here is a human infant. But what does your faith tell you?

Who is This whom they have laid in the manger? It is verily and indeed "the CHRIST, the LORD." It is the Eternal Word by Whom all things were made. It is the Second Person of the Supreme Godhead,—GOD the SON, now Incarnate, now made in our human nature, now born into our human family of the Blessed Virgin Mary.

Here is the inward and invisible greatness of the stupendous Mystery. Here is verily and indeed GOD the SON manifest in the flesh.

This, brethren, we may well call the most profound of all profound mysteries; the most amazing of all amazing miracles; the most great of all great Sacraments. The outward part is lowly and humble indeed,—only a little child; but the inward part is great, and amazing, and glorious, and heavenly, above and beyond all our thoughts,—for it is, in real truth, the LORD from Heaven; here is the Real Presence of GOD veiled beneath this lowly sign.

O see then, brethren, that you rightly believe and adore this stupendous Mystery of GOD and of CHRIST. Here is a little child, and yet the Mighty GOD. Here is a human infant, and yet the Maker of all things. Here is the Son of the Blessed Virgin Mary, and yet the Eternal SON of GOD Most High. Here is the Divine Presence veiled beneath this lowly form.

And now, brethren, let us call to mind the purpose for which this infinitely great Mystery is ordained. Why is GOD made Man? Why is the LORD from Heaven thus born of the Blessed Virgin Mary into our human family?

The Angel tells us all in one word: "Unto you is born this day, in the City of David, a SAVIOUR."

He Who is one with the FATHER is made also one with us, in order that He may be to us a SAVIOUR.

This is the glad tidings from Heaven; this is the Gospel, the good news, the glad tidings of great joy, for us sinners to hear.

Even this day, brethren, His own human birthday, the LORD JESUS offers Himself to every one of us to be our SAVIOUR, to be JESUS to us, for us, and in us.

To-day He presents Himself to you, brethren, in the most gentle, humble manner, so that

the most wretched sinner amongst us may be
greatly encouraged to come very near to Him
with a penitent humble believing heart, to receive His saving grace.

O how easy of access, brethren, has our SA-
VIOUR made Himself to-day, even to sinners,
even to sinners such as we are. We have not
to ascend up into the glory of the highest
heaven to worship Him in all His dreadful
Majesty; we have to go only into a cattle-shed,
and there we have to see our SAVIOUR "lying
in a manger," come down from Heaven to seek
and to save that which was lost; to save sinners, to give Himself for us, and to us, as our
SAVIOUR, even to as many as will believe in
Him and obey Him.

This is the only glad tidings for any sinner
to hear, that the Eternal SON of GOD is born
into our human family. This is the glad tidings of great joy, a joy unspeakable and full of
immortal glory; a joy that will never grow less,
never end; that GOD the SON is manifest in
the flesh, in order to be our SAVIOUR; in order
to give Himself for us, and to us, to save us
from our sins now and for ever.

O let none of us, brethren, neglect so great
salvation. O let none of us trifle with this
profound Mystery of Divine Love. O let none
of us be living as if we had never heard of the

Manger and the Cross of GOD's Eternal SON. But let us give all diligence that we may learn ever more and more to believe in GOD our SAVIOUR; to obey Him, to follow Him, to keep His Word, to honour Him, to glorify Him, and to love Him for ever.

But now, brethren, it is time for me to invite you to the true Christmas Feast. For the LORD Himself has spread a Table for you, here in the wilderness of this world, even to-day.

And here is another great Mystery of our faith. If you use your sight, your natural sense only, you might easily pass it by and say: "O there is nothing here but a little bread and wine." For the outward and visible part of the Holy Sacrament is lowly and humble; it makes no grand show, it is only of this earth.

But, brethren, if you will use your faith, your faith resting on our LORD's own words, then you will be able to discern the inward, invisible, heavenly part of this holy Mystery. For at His Table, and *only* at His Table, our LORD says to us: "Take, eat, This is My Body, This is My Blood."

Here therefore we know, by faith in our LORD's word, here is the Presence of the Body and Blood of CHRIST. And that Presence is here granted *for our participation* in a heavenly

Mystery, as S. Paul writes, "The Bread which we break, is it not the Communion of the Body of CHRIST? The Cup of blessing which we bless, is it not the Communion of the Blood of CHRIST?"

Here then, brethren, is that which is Meat indeed. Here is the Table of the LORD, from off which He feeds us with the very Living Bread of Heaven, that is with Himself. Here is a Heavenly Banquet; here is the Food of Immortality both for our bodies and our souls. Here is the Holy Communion of the Body and Blood of CHRIST. Here our SAVIOUR is ready to give Himself to us through this Holy Communion of His Living and Life-giving Body and Blood, to be in us, our very Life; if we come to this Holy Feast truly repenting of our sins, and unfeignedly believing in Him.

O then let all humble, penitent, believing, child-like, trembling sinners, draw very near to the LORD, and take this His own Holy Sacrament, kneeling down in the dust as by the very side of His lowly manger-throne at Bethlehem.

SERMON XVI.

THE DIVINE PRESENCE.

First Sunday after Christmas.

ISAIAH LX. 19.

"THY GOD THY GLORY."

IN this chapter the great Prophet prophesied of the coming of the LORD GOD in very clear and striking words. The chapter begins with a call to the Church to "arise and shine" at the coming of the LORD, at the Advent of the promised MESSIAH, at the manifestation of GOD in the flesh: "for thy Light is come, and the glory of the LORD is risen upon thee."

And then as soon as the Prophet had thus spoken of the rising of the Sun of Righteousness, he prophesies of the admission of the Gentiles into the Church, that all nations may share in the glory of His Presence, that all the

families of the earth may be blessed in Him,
saying, "And the Gentiles shall come to Thy
Light, and kings to the brightness of Thy
rising." For before the coming of the LORD
from Heaven, we Gentiles, in these distant
islands of the sea, were sitting in spiritual
darkness, "aliens from the commonwealth of
Israel, and strangers from the covenants of
promise." (Eph. ii. 12.)

But when the SON of GOD came in the flesh,
then He gave express commandment that His
Kingdom should be opened to all Nations. At
the very first moment of His Manifestation He
called the Gentile kings from the east to come
and worship Him, that they should see the
brightness of His rising, and be the first-fruits
of the whole Gentile world. Then began the
fulfilment of that prophecy, "Rejoice, ye Gentiles, with His people."

But let us now rather consider that divine
glory which the Prophet said should fill the
Church at the Advent of GOD in the flesh.
When the Messiah should come, when the
LORD from Heaven should be made the Second
Man, when the SON of GOD should be manifest
in the flesh in order to be the New Head of
our fallen race, then, the Prophet writes, our
true Light would arise, then GOD Himself
would be our glory, "thy GOD thy glory."

This, brethren, is, as S. Paul writes, "the glory that excelleth." (2 Cor. iii. 10.) This is the pre-eminent glory of the Christian dispensation, the glory of the last dispensation of the grace of God. This is the glory of the more intimate indwelling and abiding Presence of God which is now granted us in the Church of Christ.

This is the very glory which S. John beheld in the New Jerusalem, the City of the Living God, the Bride of Christ, when he beheld her beginning to come down out of Heaven to this earth. For he says, he saw the Holy City descending out of Heaven, built upon the foundations of the Twelve Apostles of the Lamb, "having the glory of God" in her.

In the Jewish dispensation, indeed, God had granted His peculiar Presence. In the wilderness the Angel of His Presence went with His people, to lead and guard them night and day; when the Temple was built on Mount Zion, the Divine Presence rested, in visible glory, between the Cherubim, over the Ark of the Covenant, so that S. Paul writes thus of the Israel of old, "To whom pertained the adoption and the glory." (Rom. ix. 3.) So that, in some true sense, the Presence of God was, even then, the glory of His people Israel.

But still more excellent things are spoken of

the true Zion, the City of the Living GOD, the Heavenly Jerusalem which is now "the Mother of us all," (Gal. iv. 26,) which is the Church of CHRIST, the Mystical Body of the SON of GOD, the very Fulness of Him Who now filleth all in all.

The glory of the Presence of GOD was great indeed, in the former dispensation of His grace; but that glory was no glory in respect of the glory which now excelleth. All was in comparative darkness before the Advent of the LORD GOD in the flesh. Then when. He was manifested, the true Sun arose; then our GOD became our glory so as He had never been before.

So the Prophet David prophesied of the times of the Messiah, saying, "Surely His salvation is nigh them that fear Him, that glory may dwell in our land." (Ps. lxxxv.) And also it is written of the Church of CHRIST, "GOD is in the midst of her." (Ps. xlvi.)

Now, therefore, in the symbolical language of the Prophets, the sun is no more needed by day, nor the moon by night; even those great lights of GOD are as nothing at all, in comparison of that glory of the Presence of our LORD which is now granted us.

Let us then very briefly call to mind, brethren, the special ways in which this prophecy is now receiving its fulfilment amongst us,—"Thy GOD, thy glory."

First of all, by the Incarnation of GOD the SON, that new Name is His, "Immanuel." GOD is with us, so as He never was before. Now the very Presence of GOD Himself is manifested in our nature; our manhood is in Him divinely glorified. He, the Eternal Word, being Himself now for ever Man, is truly our glory,—our infinite and eternal glory.

In old time they saw the glory of the LORD in the fire that consumed the Sacrifice, in the flaming bush, in the cloud of light, and on Mount Sinai, and in various occasional visitations. But to us the SON of GOD has come Himself made in our manhood, to be ever Man, our abiding Light and Life and Glory. Now our eyes have seen the salvation of GOD in no transient vision, in no figurative glory, but in His own true Person, even the Incarnate Deity.

Then, since the Incarnation of the SON of GOD, and since His Ascension into the glory of the FATHER, His Presence is granted to be not only with us, but in us, individually, so as it never was before. For He ascended in our manhood for the very end that "He might fill all things" with His Presence. Now He is given to be our New Divine indwelling, Life-giving Head. Now the Church is, what it

L

never was before, "the Body of CHRIST," the
Second Adam, "the Fulness of Him that filleth
all in all." (Eph. ii. and iv.)

Now it is said of us, as it never could have
been said of any before, "Know ye not your
own selves how that JESUS CHRIST is in you?"
(2 Cor. xiii. 5.) And, "Know ye not that your
bodies are the members of CHRIST?" (1 Cor.
vi. 15.) Now also we are fed with the spiritual
food of the Living and Life-giving Body and
Blood of CHRIST, by which Holy Communion
we are made one with Him; for by these Divine
Gifts the LORD Incarnate comes to dwell in us,
according to His own sure words, "He that
eateth My Flesh and drinketh My Blood dwelleth in Me and I in him."

The glory of the Presence of GOD with His
people of old, then, brethren, was no glory, in
comparison of this His indwelling abiding
Presence in us now, since the Incarnation of
His SON and the coming of the HOLY GHOST.

Now it is true for us, so as it never was for
any before the coming of our LORD GOD in the
flesh,—"Thy GOD, thy glory."

Now is fulfilled for us all that was spoken of
by the prophecies of old concerning the Presence of GOD: "I will dwell in them, and
walk in them."

It only remains therefore that we should

very earnestly ask ourselves, how we are profiting by our greater and higher gifts of grace in the kingdom of God Incarnate.

Are you giving all diligence, brethren, to live no longer according to the flesh, but according to the Spirit of life in CHRIST JESUS? Are you walking worthy of your vocation as members of the Church of CHRIST, temples of the HOLY GHOST, partakers of the Body and Blood of the SON of GOD, heirs with Him of the glory of GOD? Are you remembering, daily, Whose you are, Who dwells in you, Who is watching you, Who is striving with your hearts, Who is loving you, to what glory and virtue you are called? Do you know that you can do all things through Him Who dwelleth in you? O do not think that any degrees of holiness are beyond your reach. O do not stop short in any of your aims and ventures of faith. O be not content with any attainment you have yet made. O fill up all your time with works of faith and labours of love for His Name's sake. Do all unto the LORD JESUS. See that you become rich in good works, like a tree in a good soil laden with fruit, "filled with the fruits of righteousness which are, by JESUS CHRIST, unto the glory and praise of GOD."

SERMON XVII.

THE PRESENT TRYING OF OUR FAITH.

First Sunday after Christmas.

S. JOHN I. 10.

"HE WAS IN THE WORLD, AND THE WORLD WAS MADE BY
HIM, AND THE WORLD KNEW HIM NOT."

WE might very naturally have expected that
when the fulness of time was come that GOD
should send forth His SON into this world, He
would have sent Him down from Heaven with
such signs of overwhelming power and resplen-
dent glory, that all the world would have been
obliged at once to know Him and to believe in
His Divine Mission. We might have supposed
that during His life upon earth no one would
ever have had occasion to say, "Who is
this?"

But in His perfect wisdom it pleased GOD
that it should not be so. This is not the way

in which God deals with us.   When the Lord came down from Heaven, He came in such exceeding great humility that the world did not know Him, did not believe Him.

Was not this strange, brethren, past all our thought?   That the Creator of the world should be living visibly in the world, and His creatures should not know Him !   Have you ever heard of anything so strange?   Can you ever think of anything so strange?   In all the books of fiction that you have ever read, have you ever read anything so surpassingly strange as this is?   That God our Saviour should so hide His Divine glory, that when the world saw Him, it did not know who He was?

But so it pleased God that it should be. So was the Prophet's saying fulfilled, in its very highest instance, " Verily Thou art a God that hidest Thyself, O God of Israel, the Saviour."   (Isaiah xlv. 15.)

Such a trying did God our Saviour appoint for the men of that generation.   He Himself dwelt among them, in such a manner that no one was forced to know Him.   Our Lord's Divine glory was so veiled beneath His human weakness, that the men of this world, judging as they do only by the outward appearance, were "offended in Him," that is, they stumbled and fell.   For they had no hearts, prepared by

faith and holiness, able to perceive in the lowly
Son of Mary the Presence of GOD.   They could
not believe that a person who seemed to be
only the Son of Joseph the carpenter, who
lived in such a humble home, who laboured in
so lowly an employment, who lived for thirty
years in such retirement, in such poverty, and
in such exceeding great humility in that despised little town of Nazareth; the world could
not believe in such a one that He was verily
and indeed the very CHRIST of GOD, the very
LORD from Heaven, the Redeemer of Israel.

Those people of Nazareth amongst whom
the LORD JESUS lived for thirty years a life of
perfect goodness, even they did not learn to
know Him.   They merely said, when they heard
anything that struck them as strange concerning Him, "Is not this the carpenter's son?"
and so they passed it by.   Some of them lived
next door to the Holy Family, and saw the
LORD Himself go in and out continually, and
yet did not perceive who He was, but passed
by Him in the rudeness of their unbelief.

The first time the LORD preached in their
synagogue, on His return from His Baptism,
their pride was so much offended by what He
said, that the whole congregation rose up and
thrust Him out, and would even have killed
Him at once, if they could.   And of His own

near relations it is said, "Neither did His brethren believe in Him."

And on one occasion, it is written, that when His friends heard of something that He had done, "they went out to lay hold on Him, for they said, He is beside Himself." They thought they ought in kind duty towards their strange relation, to put Him under restraint, as one beside Himself.

Here pause one moment, brethren, and consider what a tremendous sign is this, what a dreadful proof is this, of the immense distance to which man has fallen from GOD.

When GOD, in the Person of Him Who is the very Wisdom of GOD, was dwelling as Man among men, setting us the example of a perfect human life, the people about Him took Him for some one beside himself.

The life of GOD manifest in the flesh was so very different to their life, that they thought He must have gone out of His mind. He was counted as a fool or a madman.

Does not this help us to see, brethren, how far we have fallen from GOD; how blinded we are by this world; how dreadfully we are putting light for darkness, and darkness for light?

Brethren, will you consider for your own selves, whether you are striving to be wise with this world, or whether you are willing to be counted mad with JESUS?

Hiding His Divine glory then beneath His human weakness, coming from the despised little town of Nazaréth, making Himself of no reputation, allowing the drunkards to make their songs upon Him, submitting Himself at last to be dragged through the streets of Jerusalem in dust and blood to the most cruel and shameful of all deaths; it is perhaps a wonder that any one should have been able to believe in Him as verily and indeed the SON of GOD, the very SAVIOUR of the world. So much so, that S. Paul reckons it as one part of the great mystery of Godliness that *some* did believe, for he writes, "Great is the mystery of godliness: GOD was manifest in the flesh; justified in the Spirit; seen of Angels; preached unto the Gentiles; believed on in the world; received up into glory." Even JESUS of Nazareth, the Son of Mary, "believed on in the world," as GOD manifest in the flesh, the very LORD from Heaven, the SAVIOUR of the world.

But these believers were so few in comparison of the rest, that the Prophet Isaiah speaks of them as almost none at all, saying, "Who hath believed our report?" scarcely any one. "To whom is the arm of the LORD revealed?" scarcely to any one.

And what was the reason that He Who made the world should be thus in the world, and yet be unknown, not believed in ?

Because He grew up, as the Prophet said, "as a tender plant," not a strong handsome plant in the eyes of the world, but as a poor weak tender sickly plant, even like a plant or a root which grows up "out of a dry ground," having no strength or beauty in the estimation of the world, but overlooked and rejected as good for nothing.

But a few, of humble hearts, taught by God, living in faith and holiness, learnt to believe in Him. To a few who were walking by faith in God, "the arm of the Lord," that is the power of God, was revealed in the Person of Jesus of Nazareth. By His mighty miracles, and by His gracious words, their faith in Him was kindled, and that faith grew and increased till it became the new strong mainspring of their life. They first believed, and then believing, they learnt to love. The love of Jesus so constrained them, that they forsook all beside to follow Him. They ventured everything for time and for eternity, on His word, on His power, on His love.

And now let us consider, brethren, that the very same kind of trying is going on still. By the thoughtless, careless multitude, who

love their life in this world, who are living for
this present world, not for God, the Lord
Jesus is still unknown, disesteemed, passed by
in rude ignorance, and rejected.   The Prophet's
words of astonishment are still receiving their
fulfilment: "Who hath believed our report?
To whom is the arm of the Lord revealed?"
Who believes the report concerning God manifest in the flesh?   Who believes in Jesus of
Nazareth, the Son of Mary, the Incarnate Son
of God?   He is still in the world, and the
world was made by Him, and the world knows
not His Presence.

Are you, brethren, learning the great lesson
of your present life-time, even to discern the
glory of God in the face of Jesus Christ?

Is the report you hear concerning His
Nativity, His Life on earth, His Cross and
Passion, His Resurrection, and His Ascension,
sinking down into your hearts, and moving you
to newness of life?   Is your faith in Jesus
the Son of God beginning to be the new strong
mainspring of your life; the very strength of
your mind, the very joy of your heart?

And here we should certainly call to mind
that very special truth concerning the Presence
of the Lord Jesus, which is now trying all of
us.   For as He Himself once lived visibly in
the world, so He has remained in the world

ever since, although not as visibly, yet as truly. He did not take leave of the world, on His Ascension to the throne of His Kingdom. That going away was only a preliminary step to His coming again to be with us in a more intimate manner. He ascended, not to be absent from us, but, as S. Paul declares, quite on the contrary, for the very purpose, "that He might fill all things with His Presence."

And He has Himself instituted a very special channel through which He communicates this His indwelling Presence to us.

In the Holy Sacrament of the Eucharist, the LORD makes good His own words, "This is My Body : this is My Blood;" and through the communication of these Divine Gifts to us, He gives Himself to us, to be in us, so as He does in no other way, and at no other time.

For here our LORD expressly and certainly teaches us, saying, "He that eateth My Flesh and drinketh My Blood, dwelleth in Me and I in him."

Here therefore is the Presence of the living Body and Blood of the LORD, and that for our very participation ; in order that hereby we may receive His own indwelling Presence, as our very Life and Glory.

But who believes our report concerning this Mystery of the Kingdom of CHRIST?

No; as it was at first so it has been ever
since. As the LORD came into the world, and
the world knew Him not, but passed by Him
in rude unbelief; so the LORD has remained
in the world, by the communication of this
Sacrament, and yet He is not understood, He
is not esteemed, He is passed by in the rudeness of unbelief.

The world is still offended at the weakness
of the outward sign of the LORD's Presence.
The signs of His Presence are not such as
force any one to discern Him. The world
passes by in unconcern and learns nothing.

Naaman was much too proud to go down to
that little silent stream of Israel to find the
healing Presence of the Power of GOD. So the
world still is much too proud in its unbelief to
seek for the healing Power of the Presence of
the LORD JESUS in His Sacraments.

When those people of Nazareth saw the
LORD JESUS working in that carpenter's shop,
they were offended, and said, "O, it's only a
poor man, working at his daily labour." So
now when they see only some bread on the
LORD's table, they pass by in unbelief, and
say, " O, it's only a little piece of bread. The
Presence of the LORD's Body surely cannot be
there !"

Yet the LORD's own words are just as plain,

and certain, and clear, as the sun in the sky, "This is My Body." At His own Holy Table, and nowhere else, does the LORD JESUS speak these words to us; and yet, "Who believes our report?"

The same Body of GOD Incarnate which was born of the Blessed Virgin, the same Body which now is seated in power and glory at GOD's right hand, is now also present on our altar; but who believes it?

The world ridicules the very idea. The world loudly contradicts. The world still passes by the Presence of the Body of the SON of GOD in the rudeness of unbelief, and reviles those who adore It.

The same kind of trying is going on then still, brethren. The Signs of the Presence of our LORD are not grand and overpowering. No, His Presence can only be discerned by humble faith.

Here, if time permitted, we might well consider that there is another similar instance of this kind of trying of us all, caused by the Presence of the Kingdom of CHRIST amongst us. As CHRIST Himself was at first present in the world, so now is His New Kingdom. He Himself is reigning on the Throne of that Kingdom which He received of the FATHER on His Ascension; but this His new Kingdom reaches down to this world, and is now among us, and is administered by the Bishops, the successors of the Apostles. They have the keys of the Kingdom in their keeping. Their spiritual power exceeds infinitely in glory all the secular power of the Civil Ruler.

So that this forms of necessity a trial for all of us, whether we will discern the Presence of this Kingdom of the Lord Jesus; whether we will live as obedient subjects of His Kingdom, understanding its mysteries, hoping in its glory. Who of us believes in this Kingdom? Who of us discerns its Presence? Who understands that the Holy Catholic Church, built on the Foundation of the Twelve Apostles of the Lamb, is the very Kingdom of the Lord Christ upon earth?

The world knows it not, nor believes it for an instant, but ridicules it.

Brethren, the hiding of the Presence of the Lord Jesus and of His Kingdom under lowly signs is still forming a great part of our trying before God.

The entrance into our Lord's New Kingdom by one Sacrament, and our continuance in it by the other, is a great trying of us. This is God's way of dealing with us.

The Church is the Fulness of Christ; His Presence is now extended throughout the whole Body of His Church; but we may live all our life long and not find it out, just as those people at Nazareth lived close to the LORD,.and never found out who He was. We may be like blind men, not seeing the light of the noonday sun.

O consider, brethren, what is your faith in the LORD JESUS? What is your faith in the mysteries of His Kingdom? Is it beginning to be the new, strong mainspring of your heart and life, so that you are venturing everything on His word, for time and for eternity?

Remember, it is one part of the character of the ungodly; "As for the Mysteries of GOD, they knew them not." (Wisdom ii. 22.)

J. MASTERS & Co., Printers, Albion Buildings, Bartholomew Close.

www.ingramcontent.com/pod-product-compliance
Lightning Source LLC
Chambersburg PA
CBHW020544270326
41927CB00006B/716